# B I C Y C L E S ,   C A N O E S ,   D R U M S

New and Selected Poems

Dan Sklar

Ibbetson Street Press
25 School Street
Somerville Massachusetts 02143

Ibbetson Street Press
25 School Street
Somerville Massachusetts 02143
617-628-2313

ISBN 978-0-615-24473-0

for Denise and Max and Sam

Acknowledgements

Special thanks to Doug Holder, Harris Gardner, Bill Harney, Maggie Harney, Enid Larsen, Angela Licciardo, Sean Teaford, Ruth Henderson, G. Tod Slone, Sara Quay, Laura Rossi-Le, my family, and my colleagues, friends, and students at Endicott College. I could not have done this without their enthusiasm and encouragement.

Some poems in this collection first appeared in the following publications. The American Dissident, Amoskeag, Atlanta Review, Barbaric Yawp, Buckle &, bowwow, Chase Park, English Journal, Familiar, Free Verse, Genie: 2, Harvard Review, Ibbetson Street Press, The Iconoclast, July Literary Press, Lalitamba, Main Channel Voices, Main Street Rag, Marginalia, Mid-America Poetry Review, Minnetonka Review, New York Quarterly, Orbis, Poetry East, Potomac Review, Rhino, Rio Grande Review, Slab, Soundings, Square Lake, Steam Ticket, Urban Spaghetti, Willow Review, and Zone 3.

Cover design by Angela Licciardo

Artwork by Dan Sklar

"It's a poem because I wrote it."

--Frank O'Hara

"Be radical, be radical; but not too damn radical."

--Walt Whitman

"The arguments against free verse are old, but not as old as free verse."

--Carl Sandburg

# INTRODUCTION

# Contents

Here are poems that are grounded in three basic themes: work, writing, and family. What I am after is freedom, spontaneity, and the naturalness of language in writing. The chief concerns of these poems are sincerity and an open and clear voice. I do not want these poems to be something separate from life. I write in a simple and direct way; if I like a phrase I repeat it because I like it. I may even use the same line in more than one poem, the way we say the same things to people.

Poems ought to be like life--wild and sad and funny and serious and tragic, and in some way all of these things at once. A poet is a reporter and the world is the beat. I write in a journal every day, recording experiences, observations, what I see, hear, think, remember, and feel. I do not set out to write a poem, but later on when I read through the journal I find poems I did not know I had written. On occasion I will see a poem happen, like "Sam Listens," which I wrote exactly as I saw it.

I take seriously what Ezra Pound said, "make poetry new." I do not want to write like anyone else, if that's possible. I want to create new forms of poetry. Sure, I have been influenced by many writers who write differently than I do, whether it is in style, theme, or topics, but I respect all forms and styles of poetry. I am experimenting all the time. Each time I write, it is as if it is my first time, like I have not done it before. The poem, and the way it is put together, becomes the object I am writing about as well as the subject. The way the poem is written is part of its meaning. All of it, I feel, comes from a deep and original, and yet common, place. I write to try to understand myself and the world and to question the things we just assume to be true, but mostly I write to remember the brightness of being alive.

Read these poems like riding a bicycle and looking all around, singing. Read these poems like drifting in a canoe under the sky, the earth holding you up, flying. Read these poems like playing drums, the rhythm and beat of drums talking the language of drums.

--Dan Sklar

BECAUSE

I don't want to understand things,
I want to love them.
Even though it is no use,
I will keep trying.

I think people should be free
because when goofy people
find each other
it is a beautiful thing.

I have impulses to tell you
these things and one of them
is some people look like they
come from Manhattan and
sometimes I want to do something
where I have to ride a camel
for long distances.

You know, in writing I think that
it doesn't have to be the perfect word
or even the right word—a good word
will do.

Kids should spend more time in
the adult world and if school is
going to knock the free-spirited
wildness out of my kids—I am going
to put it back in them.

Sometimes I feel like I am eating

. . .

vanilla pudding in the dark.

I always feel healthy and good
and clean when I am writing.

I am glad Sam plays the flute
like Thoreau.

Thoreau liked cats for their freedom.

I am glad Max plays the saxophone
like Johnny Hodges.

I don't know what Hodges thought
about cats.

The Bronze Age was 3000 years ago.
CHANGES

I am deluded this way
I actually think I can
write poetry and that
I am going to be a great
playwright at least I am
certain I am not going to
write a novel because
I cannot make things
up everything I write
is true and I don't
change what is true
and it gets me in trouble
sometimes and I say
things that get me
in trouble when I should
say nothing at all I don't
say nothing enough
I have to learn how to
say nothing more and I
do not want to say
obvious things or pretend
I am one way when
I am not that way
at all but I am crazy
this way and like it I
hold a grudge real bad
for a time then one day
for no reason I am over
it and inside I remember
I remember everything
like the time I played
doctor with Louise when
I was eight and we were
in a neighbor's hammock
and I really liked what I saw
but when I got home I
thought everyone knew

• • •

and I felt guilty about it.
My mother was cooking.
My father was in the garden.
My brothers were building
a go-cart. I thought they
all knew. I hung around
them waiting for a sign.
No one said anything about it.
That night in bed
I thought about Louise
and what I saw--and thought
that it was really good and
something I would like to explore.

# WHAT I WANT

Sometimes
I want
to be out
of touch.
I do not
want to
know what
is going on.
I do not want
information
and I do not
want to give
information.
I don't want
information--
I want
relationships.
I do not
want to
believe
one thing.
There are
too many
things to
believe.
I don't want
to be more
productive.
I want to
walk across
Spain,
to come to
some little
town where
men drink
small glasses
of beer
at a café
and sweat.

# BRIDGE

In 1963, my mother's boyfriend
owned a night club.
Some of his jaw was shot off
and put back during WWII.
He had good  tough looking
scars. He and my mother
used to come in after I was
asleep and wake me. Our wirehaired
terrier barked and growled,
ran around and nipped
at his cuffs. My mother and
her boyfriend were always
very smiley and happy
and giddy--his scar
shining. I could smell scotch
and cigarettes on him,
the waxy smell  of the deep
red lipstick on her lips.
She loved to play  bridge.
He didn't play bridge.
But it was a big party whenever
they were together. I was ten.
I had a Ludwig drum set
in the corner of the living
room. I played drums to
Nat King Cole and Sinatra
and Ella Fitzgerald records.
Some Sunday afternoons
I would put on Count Basie
and play the drums along.
They sat on the couch, arms
over each others shoulders--
high ball in his hand.
I loved to play for them
because they were so happy.

One time my mother went
to get more drinks. He smiled
and said that I should also
learn how to play the bass
because jazz groups always
need bass players and that
there aren't enough bass
players around and I would
always find work as a bass
player. My mother, looking like
a cheerful Joan Crawford, came
back with the drinks
and sat next to him and
they put their arms around
each other and kissed
passionately. I liked to see
my mother happy.
It was a time of jazz and
drums and high balls and
scars and mother and happiness
and late nights and a wild dog.
A year later my mother
married a man she loved, a
radiologist who played bridge
and loved her and a boy and
a wild dog and a set of drums

# GOOD WORK

It is good to
have a job
in which you
have to ride
your bicycle
someplace
and take out
a notebook
—write things
in it and make
some sketches
as you look
something over
under trees
and sky
—write a few
more notes,
another sketch.
Then you close
the notebook,
put it in your
backpack,
buckle the straps,
get on your bicycle
and ride home.

# THOUGHTS AT A
# COLLEGE DIVISION MEETING

International issues in our courses?
I guess it's international love in mine
considering I teach poetry. I count
the years until I retire—fifteen,
when they talk about educational
technology management systems
(face to face teaching—I must not
forget about academic freedom)
and I start to dream of you and me
in a canoe on the river or on the beach—
Montauk—bicycles—drums—Indians.
I am falling asleep inside me.
Even her beautiful legs don't wake me—
and her neck and jaw and mouth and
shoulders aren't doing it to me today.
I mean, I come to these meetings to
look at her—today, nothing.
There's nothing less sexy than division
meetings  where so little is at stake.

# HOW NOT TO LISTEN

I managed to stop listening
at the funeral yesterday.
It wasn't easy, but I pulled
it off after a while, while
the priest was talking.
I realized it's actually
easier to listen than not.
I let my mind wander.
I looked around at the
statues of the saints,
their Mediterranean faces
and pious expressions.
I left my mind alone.
I started thinking my own
thoughts about death
and everlasting life
and what happens
to the soul after death.
Maybe the priest was right
about the great mystery. But
I refuse to worship death.
My wife's aunt had died.
She smoked like mad
and never believed
cigarettes had anything
to do with the emphysema
that killed her.
Her son said now Angie
would be with Frank
in heaven and he hoped
there is bingo there
so she will have
something to do while
Frank is at the track.

# BOOKS

I give my books away, now
is the time to give things away.
Students come to my office
and they leave with armloads
of books--Katherine Mansfield,
Complete Emily Dickinson,
The Norton Anthology of
English Literature.... They walk
out with the book shelves.
I throw away entire file
cabinets of papers  without
even looking through them--
it doesn't matter. I drop off
boxes of books to dusty
Methodist thrift shops. I don't care
that Stanislavski and Chekhov
and Dickens and Twain and
Ferlinghetti wrote them, old
rhetoric books--Mortimer Adler,
S. I. Hayakawa, Public Speaking
with the photo of Wendell Wilke,
Scott Nearing and Camus books.
I read them--it is time.
I give some books to my sons.
Don Quixote, Sir Gawain
and the Green Knight, Beowulf,
All Quiet on the Western Front,
Lord of the Flies, Catcher in the Rye,
Hemingway, Shakespeare, Saroyan,
1984. They read them. I keep Frank O'Hara.
I cancel my subscriptions to Poetry,
American Poetry Review, Harpers,
The New Yorker, Poets and Writers;
and get one magazine only--Ski Magazine.
Don't get me wrong, there are new
books I want to read like,
Why Sinatra Matters.
When I was in my twenties,
old guys gave me their books
and I thought they were crazy—
these are great books!
Now I'm one of those old guys
with too many things in my pockets.

# FREE VERSE OR
# I'LL TAKE THE COYOTES

I don't need complicated poems
to make me pay attention.
I don't need to read words like
myriad and austere and dearth
to make me think.
I pay attention and I think plenty.
I don't need SAT vocabulary words
in the poems I read. I don't need
to have to figure out a poem.
I'm busy trying to figure out life.
I don't need extra things to figure
out. What do I want from a poem?
One thing is, I don't want literature.
Literature is literature—not life.
Life is how Max, 15, comes home
from school looking intense—
the air steaming around him.
He can't talk about it.
He goes outside and stands
in the backyard then he lies in
the hammock.  It's cold and clear
and February.  I say let's go
for a walk. We walk over to
the elementary school to
pick up the homework Sam forgot.
We go to the grocery store and on
the way Max tells me I won't
understand.  I say it doesn't matter
if I understand or not.  He tells me
all of it.  At the store he says he's
got to get some kind of tea he's
never had before. He grabs this
tea this Hu Kwa tea and it smells
like pine tar  and it tastes like
pine tar and reminds me of how I
burned pine tar into my cross-country
skis when I was in college.
Poetry is how Max uses the word
"apparently" and wears my old blazer
and loafers and shirts and speaks Spanish
and plays saxophone and acts in
Shakespeare plays and fences.
Poetry is Sam in my old hat and vest
for his character report on Henry

David Thoreau who said:
"Live your life, do your work,
then take your hat."
Poetry is the fact that Max wants
to wear his pith helmet to a
Hawaiian dance in Boston.
Poetry is my students laughing
at my Senryu and remarks
and eating in class.
The fact of thirty college students
laughing like mad is poetry.
I want poetry straightforward—
no hidden meanings. There are
enough hidden things in this
world.  A poet is nature.
I want poetry shaped by
the jump and beat of life—
not literature. Carl Sandburg said:
"The arguments against free verse
are old, but not as old as free verse."
Thoreau said poetry was about
the commonest things—that it was
nothing but healthy speech.
William Stafford said that in his
area coyotes are the best poets.
I'll take the coyotes. I say
a poet is a reporter
and the world is the beat.
I say poetry is how Max has to have
some different kind of tea he's
never had before and it smells
and tastes like pine tar.
But that's just my humble opinion.

# ANYTHING WITH HORSES

Any movie with horses.
Anything where there isn't much talk.
Anything with Mexican bandits
and Mexican girls in a saloon.
Anything with flying.
Movies with characters searching
for something.
Any rounding up of characters
for a heist.
Any movie where characters say
"I reckon."
Anything where you know where
something is but the
characters don't.
Any movie where people
wear sombreros
and ponchos and sweat.
Anything with violins and jazz music.
Anything where a character has to
think hard about something.
Anything where a guy
never loosens his tie.
Anything with old things.
Anything in black and white.
Any movie with people who
don't want to talk about something--
the scene ends before they do.
Any movie where characters
have to wait for something and keep
checking their watch.
Any movie where
characters have a drink,
look at each other
and know something
and that is enough.
Anything with a wise guy kid
and a tough gambler stuck
with each other.
Anything where a guy's wife
is going crazy and he still loves her.
Anything Japanese where characters
eat rice in a hut and it's raining.
Anything with a guy in his office
late at night and a woman comes in.
Anything where a character

rides fast up to a saloon,
hitches his horse to a post,
goes in, drinks a whiskey, turns
around and is shot dead.
Any rooftop chase.
The Sahara Desert.
Anything with spies. Morocco!
Anything with secret messages.
Anything with a midnight meeting
in a café where people
speak French.
Anything with fishing.
Anything with passports.
Anything with a bicycle.
Anything with an Alfa Romeo.
Anything with someone running.
Anything with a jazz club.
Anything with safecracking.
Anything with an immigrant
looking at the Statue of Liberty.
Anything where a character is
packing a suitcase in a mad dash.
Anything where a character calls
the other lead, lady.
Anything where a guy is eating
a sandwich in a car.
Anything where characters sneak in
dark places that have walls of little
blinking lights, dials, knobs,
buttons and levers.
Anything with clicking things with
red numbers that count down
and beep.
Anything with things that click
and snap together.
Anything in Italy.
Anything with nomads and gypsies.

. . .

Anything with rebels!
Anything with horses.
Anything with two characters arguing
and when they're not arguing
they're kissing.

# WORKING

When you are seen
working it is good.
I want to be seen
mowing the lawn
in the summer
and raking the leaves
in the fall.
Jack said he drove by
and saw me raking
the leaves on Thursday
and I was thinking,
yes that is good
that Jack saw me
raking the leaves.
I want to be seen
shoveling snow
and planting apple trees
and pulling weeds
from the walk and patio.
I want my neighbors
to see me working
outdoors and riding
my bicycle
to the grocery store
and picking blueberries
from the bushes
in the backyard
and setting up
the ladder and
cleaning leaves out
of the gutters
and using the
wheelbarrow to move
things from one place
to another.
I want to be seen working.
I want people to say
I saw you yesterday
digging
in your front yard.
It's no good lying
in the hammock
disappearing
into dreams.

# MYTHOLOGY

In mythology, Helen is lonely
because the more beautiful
you are, the lonelier you are.
Even though swords plunge
into men and blood soaks
the sand--Helen, in her
rooms with maids and rugs,
is lonely.
It is lonely to live in a man's
mind. A red cat can rub
against her. A man can
come sweating, and
sweating, sweat on her
sheets. It is lonely to be
Helen--living in the
imagination of men.
Ships creak, great
ocean rocks vaulting
to the sky--the tides and
sun and voices.
Helen is lonely.
She does not like to see
men weeping--the moon.
She wanted to go.
She had a big ego--knew
she was beautiful. Paris
gave her what she wanted
--romance. You cannot
expect romance from a good
soldier like Menelaus,
let's face it. To love a
beautiful woman takes time.
Helen loved men and the
things about them--flirted
with Odysseus. No one is
above flirting. Although the
stories do not say it, you
cannot tell me Odysseus
did not often think about
the smooth, soft inside
skin of Helen's thighs,
and to the place where
her long legs lead.

# A DREAM

Sometimes
when it
is raining
late at night
I fall asleep
in the chair
and dream
that women
are kissing
my face
like a
thousand
cool
raindrops.

# I NEED TO LOOK AT THE MOON

I heard kids playing football
in the park one November
night and wondered if the coaches
ever stop them to look at the moon
and why they don't look at the moon
and if after the game, walking to the car
their mother or father says,
"Look at the moon.
It's a crescent moon tonight. "
I mean it is important for kids
to crash into each other,
but so is looking at the moon.

# JAZZ SONG

She is a jazz Song
She is a blues jazz song
A tall jazz song
A slow jazz song
A slow jazz torch song
She is a torch song
She is a long jazz torch song
you do not want to end.
She is a night blonde
jazz song in a black dress.
She is a long blonde
jazz song at a table
with a white table cloth
and a scotch and soda.
A cool slim sax jazz song
A slow bass solo song
She is soft brushes on a
high-hat, ride cymbal,
slow drum solo song.
She is an I been carrying
a torch for you jazz song.
I love the word torch--
it says it.
She is a slow cool
drum solo in a beautiful
drunken jazz night.

# A MOVIE

I would like
to be
in a movie
where I ride
a horse fast
through the night
over fields
and woods
and streams
and wooden bridges.
I want to sweat
and I want the
horse to sweat
and breathe
so you can hear it.
I want to ride up to
an old cottage
at the top
of a hill
where you sleep
in white sheets--
your bed
like a cloud.

# FAMOUS POETS

I don't dig
rhyming poems
about God.
I can't tell you
why exactly,
even when they
have irony
and insects
and such.
Oh, I know
some of the
poets are
great poets
and the poems
are considered
good because
famous poets
wrote them,
but God is
too big
for rhyming
poems, and too
small too.
There is something
sick about
rhyming poems
about the holocaust.
Unless a little kid
wrote it.
When I die
I would hate it
if someone wrote
a rhyming poem
about me.
Just put a hat on me
send me drifting
in a canoe.

## HOW IT IS

Don't be profound.
Don't be insightful.
You don't have to laugh.
You don't have to talk.
You don't have to say
obvious things
or pretend to be sincere.
You don't have to
follow the rules
of writing at all.
Write run-on sentences.
Ever read
Walt Whitman—
Henry David Thoreau?
There is a man in this
café knitting an orange
sweater for his niece.
He's got a dagger tattoo
on his forearm and he
drinks coffee through a
straw from a plastic mug.
You don't have to go
to college.
You could learn how
to repair saxophones
or rebuild accordions
or cook. College is all
just paper.
Sometimes I wonder
how I got so lucky to
marry a beautiful
woman and then I
see other beautiful
women and their goofy
husbands
and I see how it is.

# SAM THE GYPSY

It occurred to me
that Sammy is a gypsy boy.

I was reading about gypsy
children and figured out he
could be a good one.

He doesn't want to be told
not to be late for breakfast.

He doesn't want to wear
socks and shoes.

He doesn't want to be told when
to go to sleep.

"I want to stay up with you, Dad,"
he says on the edge of dreams
in his white bed.

He wants to be wild and keep being wild.

The thing he loves most is freedom
and to be with someone and to sing
and play music and wear brightly
colored clothes.

O, we should have been gypsies,
I 'd play a drum, and Denise would dance

and tell fortunes the people
would believe
because they are true
and she knows
and she is beautiful and

Max would play saxophone
and Sam would dance too.
We would be happy with music
in the outdoors of the world.

# THOREAU THINKING

At dinner with Hawthorne
Thoreau was thinking,
I will take this man up the river
in my canoe and I will show him
how Indians paddle.
He will buy the canoe.
I will build another.
Thoreau sold Hawthorne
a canoe which Thoreau
had "built by his own hands."

The quote is from Nathaniel Hawthorne's journal dated September 1, 1842.

# WHAT THOREAU WAS WORRIED ABOUT

Ever notice how
Henry David Thoreau
always looks worried
in the photograph--
worried and formal.
This is what Thoreau
was worried about:
1. Getting his own place.
2. Getting out of his parents'
boarding house.
3. Writing something the way he
wanted to write which would also
sell.
4. Getting out of the pencil business.
5. The pain in his lungs.
6. Getting laid.
7. The state of society and excess
of materialism and what it does
to nature and how humans need
to somehow live in harmony with
nature.
8. The preservation of wildness.
9. The campfire he and a friend
started that got out of control and
spread for a hundred acres in
Concord.  It was a big joke around town.
10. His canoe.

# THE LOBSTER MEN

I walked down to the harbor in Marblehead and saw the lobster men working. One was loading lobster traps on to a conveyor belt up to the pier from a floating dock. Another lobster man was stacking them in a pile beside a green pick-up truck. He was talking to a small boy as he did this, without missing a beat, and smiling. I couldn't hear what he was saying. Soon the boy walked away with his mother. Both men wore blue jeans, blue sweatshirts, baseball caps, and thick work gloves. They were tall, broad men who looked like they were in their late fifties. The October afternoon was cool and sunny. The tide was high. The conveyor belt had a lazy squeak which was almost pleasant. The man on the floating dock steadily loaded the lobster traps, one at a time, and the man on top took them off as they reached the top. They both moved at an even pace. When that was done, the other man went up the ramp and began handing the traps to the man who had climbed on to the flatbed of the truck. The man on the truck stacked the traps in neat wedges and straight and side-ways geometrical patterns to fit them on snuggly. Each lobster trap had a rope and buoy inside. The man jumped down and put the last trap on the truck, shoved it in, and gave it a pat. They got into the truck, started it, and drove away. The traps looked heavy and the work looked hard. They did not talk. They seemed used to it. They actually appeared to be downright cheerful doing it. They seemed happy. They seemed to like each other. There was a wonderful plainness in what they were doing. They seemed to have easy, pleas-ant feelings toward each other. It was just two lobstermen working together moving lobster traps from one place to another. There were no arguments about whether literary theory should be a required course in some little college somewhere. There was no discussion on how a piece of literature should or should not be read. These men were loading lobster traps and that was all that mattered.

I had walked down to the pier after taking my son to Shakespeare Acting class. I saw these men working and watched them and started thinking about them. I did not know the complications in their lives at home. For the time I saw them, they were just men loading lobster traps in a truck--only men and lobster traps and a pick-up truck on a golden October day. That moment, that place, those men are the stuff of literature. Who are their wives? What are they like? Are they big smiley blondes or slim cool brunettes? How did they meet? Have they any children? Have their children grown up and become me-chanics or teachers? Who are their friends? Have they been di-vorced? Do they go to church? Will they have a beer together in a bar after unloading the lobster traps in their backyard? Will they work out on a piece of paper the costs and expenses and sales and profits of catching and selling lobsters and then fold the piece of paper and put it in a pocket and later in a folder?  Will the same thick fingers that wrote the numbers on a piece of paper with a short pencil, the same hands that hauled lobster traps from the harbor and put them on a boat, carried them to a conveyor belt, threw them on a truck--will those hands later touch the smooth soft skin on the hips of a woman?

# WE SAY THESE THINGS

Max says
there are
enough cars
on the road.
There are
not enough
birds
and trees, but
there are
enough cars.
There are
enough
Wal-Marts.
There are
not enough
small farms
and small stores
and small
restaurants
and bicycle riders
and small schools
and windmills
and accordions,
but there
are enough
Ramada Inns.
There is not
enough wildness.
My last pen
just ran
out of ink
and I love
running
out of
envelopes
and when
I have
filled another
Composition
Notebook.

# PENELOPE

When I am through
I will get a rowboat
and a small lobster
boat  named
Penelope
and some
lobster traps—
check the traps
every day and
give the lobsters
away and ride
my bicycle
home
and read
travel books—
one about Italy.

# IT IS GOOD TO BE A NUMBER

It is good to be a number.
It is easier when you see the moon.
You can sit on the couch and a red cat
will leap into your lap as you read a book.
It is all a matter of math.
Your behavior is like one in love.
You don't have to think about it when you're a number.
Then it will not matter about the moon.
A train goes past at dawn, a cat
looks up and you look up from your book.
You are figuring out the math
that is your behavior in love.
This fact concerns your number.
When you are alone you are a number.
It makes it easier to look at the moon.
You can give a number to a cat
and the cat can walk across your book.
The arrival of the train is a matter of math.
People read books on the train about love.
It is easier to be in love with a number.
It is good to be a cat with a number.

# WHAT I LIKE ABOUT BASEBALL

I like baseball better
than poetry.
I would rather see
a baseball game
than go to a poetry reading.
Baseball is more Zen
than poetry.
I like when a guy gets a double
and when he reaches
second base a split second
before the second
baseman gets the throw
from right field and even
though the batter
stands on second, the second
baseman tags him anyway
and they both smile.
I like when players
on opposite
teams smile at each other.
I like how in baseball
no one has to talk.
You can play a whole game
and not say a word.
I like all the signals.
Sometimes signals
are better than words.
Sometimes the catcher or
pitching coach or
manager or
some other player
will run up
to the pitcher
and say something.

The pitcher will nod.
I like when after two strikes
in a tight situation
the catcher will
run to the pitcher,
say something,
run back, and the pitcher
immediately throws the ball
and the batter swings
and misses
and you don't know
what the catcher said
but it worked.

# WHEN

Who drives the trucks
that deliver the
machine guns?
Who is the pilot
of the plane that
delivers
the ammunition?
Who inspects the
boxes of bullets
in the factory?
What does he think
about when sipping
coffee before work?
Putting on his coat?
Getting in his car?
Turning the key?
What happens to
the owner of the
gun manufacturing
corporation when he
comes home and
gets on the floor
to play with his
children?
Does he think
it is a good
world filled
with all kinds
of children
dancing.
What about that
Matisse
in the living room
he bought with
the money he made
selling the rifle
that shot the mother
and child—
the machine guns
in the hands of boys like
our boys who hold
backpacks
filled with notebooks and
Dickens and pencils?
Who are these people

. . .

whose business is
the business
of weapons?
Where do they live?
What do they think?
How come you never hear
of one having a nervous
breakdown and saying it is
wrong?  Taking land from
other humans is wrong.
Killing is wrong.
Where are the little farms?
Drums?  Dances?  Songs?
Do the daughters of the
arms dealers take clarinet
lessons and dance classes?
Do they sleep in warm beds
with white sheets?
Are they kissed and
tucked in by their mother
with a shining face?
Where are these factories?
Who are these leaders?
It happened to the
natives of the Americas,
the Armenians, the Jews,
the gypsies, the Africans—
when does it stop?
When will a leader say
no more guns?
Here are drums!
Here is a farm!
Here is a job!
Here are songs!
Here are horses!
Here are dances!
Make up your own!

# IF ONLY

If only our singing could stop the war.
If only our singing could stop the war.
If only our dancing could stop the war.
If only our dancing could stop the war.
If only our acting could stop the war.
If only our acting could stop the war.
If only our art could stop the war.
If only our art could stop the war.
If only music could stop the war.
If only music could stop the war.
If only this was so, that would be all.

# AMBITIOUS POETS

This couple I met
introduced themselves
as poets. She said,
"Hello, we're poets.
The state has given
me thirty-thousand
dollars to write
poetry and my
boyfriend just had
a poem published in
Poetry Magazine."
And I said, "Hello,
people are being
blown apart in
Iraq which is more
important than
anything I have
done or
what ever I might
consider myself."

# FOR A TIME

Sometimes I feel compelled to write but I do not know what to write
so I begin like this figuring that something will come to me and it
does this sudden interest well not so sudden interest in union ideas
and doing something for people rather than all this writing and paint-
ing and this sense of being anti-technology even though I am writ-
ing this on a computer looking at my old Royal typewriter I pull out
now and then to hear it and smell it and write with it what would
Thoreau think about a computer what I am thinking is if I could
find Whitey Bulger there's a million dollar reward I quit the band
today there are plenty of drummers around and I'm the only father
to my boys I mean there's enough music in my life enough loneliness
enough togetherness Thoreau said "It's wrong to systematize our
thought and experience Let it be as it is contradictions and all" and it
is liberty I am after even though I already have it I'm not out to lead
anybody leadership implies control I don't want to control anybody
tell them my way of doing things is anything but another way to do
things Electric screens imply control What would Walt Whitman do
with a computer you think he'd sit there and say anything different
you think he'd put his students in front of computers I tell you it's big
brother it's Orwellian it's Kafkaesque metaphorical how schools are
proud of their computer labs and make signs to tell you where they
are I mean after all they're machines Shall we meet in room 125 I
mean people are impressed with machines in educational settings how
about a cotton gin room I like machines as sculptures I like old com-
puters in the snow dirty old snow from December and it's February
now and raining and perfect February time I think this summer I will
pack the kids in the car and head north to some mountain and climb
it look at the streams and rocks and sky and stay there for a time.

# WANTED

My poems
do not win
poetry
awards
because
they are
not poems
at all.
I'd rather
find
Whitey Bulger
and get that
million buck
reward.

# THIS IS A POEM

The advertisement
for the
Indian casino
says:
"In the Mohegan
language there
are no words
for boredom."
I add to that:
"...but there are
plenty of words
for sucker."

# A LETTER

I need to think about Walt Whitman every day and I need to write a
letter to him every day because everything I write is loaded with Walt
Whitman and I need to write a letter every day to someone because
there is always someone who needs to get a letter to remind her of
Walt Whitman and I begin the letter this way:
To Whom It May Concern: I am writing to remind you about which
it is important to be reminded of and that is Walt Whitman, who told
us that there are no secrets in the universe—it's all there, you see
it when you quit looking because you don't need to look anymore
because it is all you do, look that is, and breathe in everything in the
world and love everything in the world and when you are vexed by
the world and its institutions, wonder what Walt Whitman would do,
and think of him as he might have taught school back there in old
Huntington with his feet up on the desk in front, loving the wildness
of the kids and their alarm that this schoolteacher let them be them-
selves and read to them for no other reason than to hear the words
and love the images.

Sincerely yours,
Daniel Sklar

# THE CIRCUS

Circuses are depressing.
The clowns rarely make me laugh.
They are sad mostly
and get me thinking about my life.
The acrobats seem empty.
I do not believe the sincerity
of the ringmaster.
The elephants and sleek horses
and dogs and tigers
are distracted, mechanical—
something's wrong.
The tightrope artists
and trapeze artists
have perfected their mistakes.
The beautiful girl on the
elephant seems sad.
I would rather watch a girl
alone writing in her
journal under a tree.

# A HISTORY OF TRANSPORTATION

My father drove a Cadillac
His father took the subway
His father walked
His daughter rode a white horse
Her mother walked
Her father rode a camel
His daughter walked
I ride a bicycle
My son will drive an Alfa Romeo
His son will fly
His son will ride a bicycle
I want to walk, wander,
get lost, and loaf under
a tree in a meadow.
I want to ride my bicycle
in the sun nowhere, singing.

# WHAT I THINK ABOUT SOMETIMES

I used to ride my bicycle everywhere
in Manhattan, snow, rain, I didn't care.

It was how I got around. It was stolen
from a fence in Central Park

when I met with Walter Miller about
the novel I was writing.

When your bicycle is stolen, walk.

In a former life I was a black jazz drummer—

not famous or anything—just a jazz drummer
they called when the regular drummer
couldn't make it.  My name was Felix Hodges.

I was married to this tall, thin black woman
who looked like a handsome African sculpture.

She took care of a little boy in Russell Gardens.

I got a steady job with a jazz band and we moved
to Chicago.

That is why I think about jazz and drums
and who I was in Chicago.

When your bicycle is stolen, walk.

# THERE ARE SOME THINGS
# YOU HAVE TO DO

This is the way it is when a guy says "Wanna step outside?"
You have no choice. You have to go outside and you
have to say, "All right, let's go right now." And in your
mind you are willing and ready to accept the fact that
your teeth might get knocked out and your nose busted,
or maybe since he is always a giant, he'll be slow
and lumbering and you can dive, fists flying at his face
and all the time your wife is saying, "Let's just leave."
But you cannot, it is impossible, something in your
bones and blood and brain tells you that you
have to do this thing. Your eyes tighten, your
fists become rocks, your skin and muscles harden
in a flash and the truth is you have it in you to kill
a man because you are designed that way. Your
wife hates it and loves it and hates it and loves it
and hates it and loves it and hates it and loves it.
Nine times out of ten he will back down
because he senses and sees and knows you
have snapped and someday, someday, someday,
your son will walk around your backyard
in the rain shivering and talking and grabbing
toys to mess with and will not come into the house
and he will like being wet and cold getting on his
tricycle and playing with an old fishing rod.
And someday you will be canoeing with your
boy on a river and he will not want to stop and
you two will shout at the river and trees and rocks
and sky and silence with big mouths and hats
pulled way down over your eyes and he will turn
to you and say, "This is nice, Dad, really nice."

# TEACHER, MY SON IS NOT A ROBOT

At the meeting I did not speak.
My son's teachers were not talking
about the boy I know.
They were talking about a boy
they want to be like the rest.
They talked about a boy
who is not a robot, and that
is what they want, robots.
They did not talk about the boy
who acts out the stories we read.
The red ants crawl all over him
and he is sinking in quicksand
and he is Queequeg with a shrunken
head and Pip at Magwich's death
bed and George telling Lenny about
the rabbits. So his math is not perfect
and he writes some letters backwards,
but man can he read and his poems
are poetry and they made the teachers
cry (one of them anyway).
That was all I needed to hear.

# SAM LISTENS

I want to write about Samuel
and the time he stood
on the front lawn
on a warm April day
and it was six p.m.
and there were birds
and bells and a train
whistle and bees
and a dog and an airplane
and a car and kids playing
and ball bouncing
and wind chimes
and lawn mower and distant
piano and a mother calling "Ronny!"
A hammering somewhere.
I want to write this poem to remember
the time when Sam was one year
and three months listening
to these things that
came all at once.
To see Sam in a
white tee-shirt,
white diaper, bare feet,
Finger pointing to the air,
mouth saying something.

# ACADEMIC EXCELLENCE

Academic excellence is loving your bones
and the bones of your mother.
It is the moon and moss.
Academic excellence is moss
and bones and moon and
brain that knows what it knows
and does and thinks what it wants
and what it doesn't want.
What did academic excellence mean
to your feet and bones in your feet
when you were 3 and when you
were 23 and when you were 43?
It is moss and moon and night
and knowing the difference between
machines and love and moss
and moon and bones
and Mona Lisa and Miles Davis
and poetry and machines
and bones and love
and stars and night
and stars and stars
and conga drums.
It is nothing good is ever over.
It is messing
with  your 3 year old's bare feet
as you say bears, elephants,
crocodiles, giraffes, wolves,
coyotes,  elephants, and tigers
and tigers because academic
excellence is tigers and tigers
and Louis Armstrong
and John Coltrane
and Vincent van Gogh
and Clio and Thalia and Duse
and moss and bones
and bones and moss.
and stars and love
and cigars and drums
and nights and nights
and rain and rain
and moss and bones.

# THE IMPORTANCE OF SWEAT

It is important to sweat when you write
in a dark room in a quiet house and to
sleep on the floor with your feet up on
the bed and to be in a union and stand
up for the workers and the people and
to spend time wandering the streets and
beaches and woods alone and to let
yourself go to hell and get in fights
and lose a job and lie on the floor all day
and listen to old Thelonious Monk records
and smoke cigars and stare blankly and
regret everything you ever did even the
good things and quit your childhood
because it is over and there are plenty
of new childhoods around as good or
as lousy or as lousy and as good as yours
ever was with bicycles, canoes, and drums.
It is important to be a laborer in a field
and to sweat when you write and when
you get a hundred bucks you give it away.
It is important to start two short stories
and a play and never finish them and to
write poems about your children and the
opera and the muses and the crummy rotten
way kids are treated in school and college
those dirty human factories where anything
independent is filed away like Nazis who
kept plenty of files on everyone and original
ideas are against the rules so some of the most
creative kids quit and sweat alone in rented
rooms in towns like Korea, Maine or they
go to the Canadian woods to build birch bark
canoes with the Algonquin and find someone
to love or go to Mexico to sweat and sleep
on beaches and sweat honestly on poor wages
in fields and sleep on the earth with earth
dreams and drink cold water from artesian
wells and walk with stars and stars and moon
and wind and sweat and love and earth dreams.

# WHISPER

I want
to whisper
something
to her.
Something
about her
face says
whisper
to me.

# CANOES

The Iroquois traveled in canoes
Paddles dipped into green water
Birch-bark reflected white and black.
I have been thinking about canoes
Since I drifted alone on Emerald Pond
Since I glided along the shore of Long Pond
White dots glittered across to still rocks,
To the line of deep green, thick on the edge
Where tree meets tree until death.
What is it about canoes that draws me?
As a kid I canoed down the Delaware River
We tipped it over on purpose on the rapids.
We camped on the riverbank under stars
I forget the longing in the sleeping bag.
Why are canoes on my mind?
Why do I think about canoes?
When I am late for a train to Boston
When a bill is past due
When the baby doesn't sleep nights
When I have a hundred compositions to mark?

## SHE IS

I mean female
She is female
really female
She is female
Downright female
Like Myrna Loy
female she is
Wide-faced
female. Female
All female
Real female
I'm talking
female—like
plain female
Straightforward
female
Female deluxe
bona fide female
Notarized female
Power of Attorney
female
Certified female
I mean female!
Female like
Rita Hayworth
Female like female
female as female
Louise Brooks
Female like
Josephine Baker
Female like
Female arms
Female thighs
Female shoulders
Female back.
Female moves
Female hands
Female fingers
Female skin
Female mind
Female ways
Female neck
Female neck

# MERIT PAY

If this was a book I would say
give me the lowest raise on the scale,
but this is not a book and I have
an Alfa Romeo to support.
If this was a book I would sacrifice
my raise for the good of the union.
But it is not a book and I am human.
If this was a book I would tell you
I think you are beautiful and that
I want to kiss you now because
the way you throw your head back
when you laugh and I see your long
neck and it is pink, I want to put my
lips there and feel your skin there.

# ONE GREAT POEM

I want to write one great poem
that will win one of the contests
in Poets & Writers Magazine.
They will put in a little photograph
of me, half smiling or not smiling.
(A photographer once told me that I
looked better when I did not smile.)
The magazine will write little things
about me being a promising writer
even though I am forty-five
and the promises
have already been kept.
I want to write just one great poem
that college students will either get
or not get or hate or puzzle over
and write papers about with thesis
sentences and all that and misread
and read right to help them be wise.
I want high school valedictorians
to recite it at commencements.
Everyone will nod and say,
"Yes, yes, it is so true, so true."
But they will not really be sure
they know exactly
what is true about it.
But it will sound true and they
will sense that it is true and wise.
That will be enough.
I will be asked to speak at small
colleges in Indiana
and upstate New York.
I will look for profound
things to say and read my
one great poem
and it will be enough.

# FORTY-FIVE

What is it about
being in my forties?
If forties was a color
it would be brown.
Forty-five is like new
driftwood.
It is a red tree.
It is a shovel jammed
into a pile of earth.
It is dirt.
It is the ground.
It is walking with
my hands deep
in my pockets.
It as a sliver
of forest behind
old houses.
Forty-five is a cloudy
day when the
sun comes
out sometimes.
It is the shadow
of a red car.
It is a last romance
in my mind.
It is wanting to walk
to a train station
alone and to kiss
the shoulders of
a tall woman.

## PORT WASHINGTON
## TOWN BOY

He digs worms
this morning
gets his fishing gear
from the shed and straps
it on the bicycle.
He makes two peanut butter
and jelly sandwiches
and wraps them
in wax paper.
He fills a thermos with milk
and tightens
the red cap.
He sees his father's
typewriter and the
"Indians of North America"
poster. The poster
and the typewriter have
been there
for as long as he
can remember.
He packs the lunch,
a Swiss army knife,
and The Odyssey
in a rucksack.
He rides his Robin Hood
3 speed
to the pier.
Flounders bite.
He hauls them in
and throws them
back.
He eats a sandwich
and stares at the
water and sky,
at his bicycle
at the boats out there,
the cars in town with
people thinking, thinking...
He cuts some worms,
baits the hooks,
flips out the line,
feels the tug.
School is over.
School will start again.

. . .

He thinks of his mother's
open face,
his father's strong arms.
his grandmother's fierce
loyalty.
He packs his gear
and rides to a hill
with woods from where
he can see beaches
and the sound.
He eats the other
sandwich and drinks
the milk.
He reads slowly,
sitting beside a tree
and he looks up
and sees the top
of the mast of
Odysseus' ship.

# SILENCE

I have failed
in my own silence,
in the silence
of snowshoes,
in north silence,
in canoe silence
and night's stars
winter's silence.
I have failed
in the silence
of water and sky
and voices.

# A POEM

I do not want anybody
to know my name.
I want to be an actor
in a movie drunk at a bar
because the woman I love
doesn't love me—
remember it is a movie
and I am an actor
and nobody knows
my name.
I meet a sweaty
and dirty woman.

# LITTLE POEM

I do not want
a name anymore.
I want to hear
sleeping
and rain
and spring wind
and sudden
spring rain
so cool
my name will
never matter.

# GOING TO THE OPERA

I am going to the opera.
I'm off to the opera.
She went to the opera.
He went to the opera.
The opera always seems
like a good place to be
going to and to have been
and to be there away
from someplace else.
It is good when someone
says of you that you are
at the opera or that you
have been to the opera.
Your kids can say dad
and mom went to the opera.
I mean, what is it about
the opera that it is a good
place to be going or to be
there or to have been?
For one thing, you must
take a shower before going
and put on clean clothes
and dress up very neatly.
It is good to be clean
with other clean people.
Some women wear perfume.
It smells good and reminds you
of your second grade teacher.
The men usually shave and slap
on after-shave lotion and their
face tingles to them.
I like to wear argyle socks
and a white shirt and striped
tie and blue suit like in prep
school and I am still in the
habit. Another good thing
about the opera is you go to
dinner somewhere and
the silverware sparkles and
the thick cotton napkin is heavy
on your whole lap. You go to
the opera with someone you love.
She wears a black dress and you
look at her beautiful shoulders.

# MAY 14, 2000

Max asked me
if I ever teased
a kid or stood up
for a kid.
We were driving
to my office
to print something.
I told him
I never teased
anyone and it
was the truth.
Then I said
I stood up
for a black
kid once.
I was eating a
chocolate cupcake
and a French kid
with black hair
and a high-pitched
laugh said
the cake was made
out of the black
kid's skin.
I punched the French
kid right in the face
and got in
trouble for it.
The black kid
was sad and
we never talked
about it.
Max said I did
the right thing,
but nowadays
people don't
punch kids-
they tell the teacher.

# BEAUTIFUL MYSTERY

I want my kids
to know the beauty
of the world.
The fact that
at nine years old
my son plays
Mamillius in
The Winter's Tale
means nothing
to educational
research and
analysis and testing
which do not
answer the
questions because
they are the wrong
ones and do not
have anything to
do with
the beautiful mystery
of spirit and mind.
You can organize
and categorize and
test and never see
the beautiful mystery
that cannot be
tested or organized or
categorized or researched
or analyzed or statisticized.
What is important is
what is beautiful is my
kid in a Shakespeare play
and my other kid loving
and not getting enough
of the Greek Myths and
the fact that they both
love Louis Armstrong.

# IF YOU WANT A GIRLFRIEND OR BOY-FRIEND, TAKE AN ACTING WORKSHOP

I was in this acting class in New York in 1977 and was doing a scene with an actress so we met a lot out of class in places like where she worked on West 72nd Street, her parent's apartment on the Upper East Side, her apartment in Greenwich Village where she lived with her boyfriend who was dark, wore a beret, and never smiled, and my apartment on West 82nd Street where I lived with an actor, a singer, and a dancer. We were doing a scene from Waiting for Lefty, I played a cab driver and she played my wife and I actually did drive a taxi in New York at the time. One night we were rehearsing alone in my apartment.

We did the scene and soon it was night and we didn't put the lights on and we were kissing and both of us were very excited and not thinking and we were on the floor and my hand went along her skin and under her blue jeans and I felt her down there and it was the most beautiful place to touch and I loved the feel of it and could spend a great deal of time there and I was very excited and thinking about it now I get very excited but she had a boyfriend she lived with and I didn't love her and something in my mind stopped me and I stopped doing this thing I was loving to do and she was loving it, I mean, it was a very passionate situation and I was twenty-five and easily swept up into things like this and believe me I'm no saint and I had done this type of thing before, but she had a boyfriend who wore a beret and when I met him he didn't smile at all and here she was kissing me while she lived with this boyfriend which is all right I suppose because we were all searching and maybe her boyfriend kissed other women, but something told me to stop, which wasn't easy, I just had a feeling it wasn't right and there happened to be a girl I knew I liked and we were starting to see each other and I didn't want to mess with the beginning of that relationship which incidentally was the girl I married in 1981 and we have been married ever since so the something that told me to stop was right. I jumped up and said that I had to meet some friends and didn't want to be late and she looked at me like so what.

# NO POEM HERE 2

I am going to write a poem that is no where close to being a poem. There will be nothing in it that is poetical. An airplane is flying in the sky I hear it as I type this poem that is not a poem. The sun comes in the window behind me and I can hear the radio in the kitchen. Max is sleeping upstairs. Last night at a Portuguese restaurant he told me all about Federico Lorca's New York Poems and he spoke Portuguese with the owner of the restaurant who also owns the sub shop next door and is trying to make a go of a fine restaurant. Max loves to talk about literature and politics and history and languages and plays and playwriting. I tell him you have to write your own plays to act in and your own one man shows. I write a list of the things I have to get at the store and there is no poetry in the list so I will write it here: olive oil, bread, spring water, milk, orange juice, green tea, honey, some interesting cereal, apples, and laundry detergent. I also need to return the DVD Good Night, and Good Luck (good movie by the way) we rented yesterday so Sam could hear Edward R. Murrow for a school play. It dawned on me last night that I like it better when the light comes into the room I am in from another room and I use that light and do not turn the lights on in the room I am in like hall lights and kitchen lights and any light from any room I am not in. It's the same with radios--I like hearing them from another room and there should be plenty of static--maybe even between stations. I am keeping poetry out of this because the clock is ticking and life is too important for some crafted thing while children are starving and soldiers' legs and arms are being blown off. One eight year old boy's face was burned away, so I will not craft a poem here today.

# PLACES

She lives
in the same
house she
grew up in
and rides
her bicycle
places.
When she
finished
college she
came home
and stayed
and rides
her bicycle
places.
No one
tells her
how to live.
She is happy
alone
and rides
her bicycle
to the grocery
store
and beach.
In the house
she grew up in
she does what
she loves
and if
she met
someone
to love
she would
ride her bicycle
places.
No one
tells her
how to live.

# A PLAY

I want to write
a play
about
a twenty-three-
year-old woman
who will
not conform
and get a college
education
and resume
and portfolio
and work in
some corporation
and get a car
and insurance
and marry
some idiot
who wants
to control her
and have kids
who grow up
to be like
everyone else.
She wants
to ride
her bicycle
on Cape Cod
where she lives
and write.

# I CANNOT COMPETE WITH NATURE

The earth does not explain
The earth does not prove anything
The earth does not need a resume
need a diploma
need a certification of achievement
The earth does not count anything
The earth does not need Disney
need a computer lab
The earth does not need to take a standardized test
The earth does not need a car
need to fill out an application
need a license
need equipment
need to keep records
need to remember
need beautiful things
need a credit report,
a social security number, cable TV,
The Complete Works of Shakespeare,
anything from me or Yeats or Keats or
Sandburg or Dickinson or America's
current poet laureate or any professor
from some self-important little college
The earth does not need educational
technology management instructional systems
The earth does not explain
I do not take my students outside
on sunny breezy days because
I cannot compete with the earth.

# TOO FOGGY TO BE DEAD

It's too foggy to see Shakespeare.
The boys laughed at that line.
It is too foggy to see Shakespeare
It is worth repeating.
It's too foggy to see Shakespeare.
Where can I go with it?
What can I do with it?
How can I use it?
It has gotten a laugh.
It's too foggy to see Shakespeare
this gray old November time.
It's too foggy to see Shakespeare
who kept a commonplace book
for ancient quotes.
It is ancient quotes I am after--
beautiful ancient quotes I can write.
It is too foggy to see Shakespeare.
It is ancient quotes I am after--
beautiful ancient quotes.
It is sad to be dead on a foggy day
and after your funeral everyone goes
to a rundown hall with one of those
low paneled ceilings and eat
cold cut sandwiches brought
by a cousin who owns a grocery
store and he brings his homemade
coleslaw (the specialty) and there's
a bar where you have to buy drinks
they put in plastic cups and the
bartender is new--in training--
It is too sad to be dead when it's
foggy. It is sad enough to die and
then afterwards to have the people
you loved eating roast beef sandwiches
in a beat-up hall in Lynn--really sad.
But my boys laughed at the line
on the way to Angelo's wake.
It's too foggy to see Shakespeare.
I want to write beautiful and ancient
quotes that kids can write in their
commonplace book--like Shakespeare--
when he was a kid--
like Shakespeare in the fog.

# MAY 31, 1992

A sweet voiced woman sang an Italian aria
I never heard before.
It was too beautiful to hear again.
The shortwave reception faded static-y
—came back—faded away and came back.
I liked it that way.
My son, Max, was napping.
My wife, Denise, was dancing
a Sunday matinee.
The yard was spruce, the grass coming in.
Max's sleep was deep.
I could hear his bones growing.
I thought about deep sleeps in Brooklyn
beside my father when I was eleven.
I thought about Max sleeping with
the top of his head pressed to my ribs.
I was square with my relatives.
All letters had been written and sent
and all the bills had been paid.
The song was beautiful and sad.
I will never hear it again.
When it disappeared I let it go.

# SOMETHING IMPORTANT

On this page I am going to write something important and I don't know what it will be but it will be important and it will be written in the early spring dusk and I will not turn on the lights and will let the light change as the sky and listen to the radio from the kitchen and the footsteps of Denise upstairs getting ready to go out this April Saturday night we are going to walk to the restaurant in town and the boys will come straight from wrestling in the grass and Denise will come straight from upstairs and I will come straight from typing something important on this paper and what it will mean is that a family walks to town to go to a restaurant 7 o'clock on an April Saturday night and on the way we will talk about things and laugh about things and we will not realize and we will realize we are happy.

# POEM HERE

I don't dig those poems
where a guy is working
in the garden and he's
thinking about some
lousy relationship and
the flowers and plants
and earth become like
metaphors and he
thinks of what she said
to him and what he said
to her and should have
said and his hands dig
in the earth while he's
thinking these things.

# FREE SPIRITS

Henry and Ralph used to bring
their girlfriends down to the cabin
on Walden Pond.
Henry's girl was Daisy Hawkins,
a free spirit who loved
nature and men.
She was like a wood nymph,
a hamadryad whose goddess
was Artemis.
Henry and Daisy met in the woods.
On the ground Henry loved the feel
of Daisy in his arms,
in his hands.
She smelled like the earth.
He thought of her as Gaia--
mother earth. He loved to pull
off all of her petticoats
and under things, like
stripping society
of its pretenses.
This is how Henry made love to nature.
Daisy would smile
and giggle and laugh
and look at the leaves
and blue sky, pine needles
and brown earth,
tree trunks and branches,
Henry's beard,
Henry's forehead,
Henry's shoulders,
the glittery dots on Walden Pond.
Ralph's girlfriend was Mary O'Hara,
a big red haired woman who loved to
lie naked in sunshiny meadows.
Mary and Ralph drank wine
in the woods.

He called her Persephone
and loved to put his hands
on her smooth red hips and
on her thighs and feel the hair
under her dress and put his
hands on her breasts--fingers
pressing her nipples.
He was intrigued by
the shape of a woman
and what would happen
to her body when he
touched her.
Ralph told her she was
like the earth--so beautiful
he could hardly believe
that she existed.

# I MEAN IT

I could live in
a third-world
country.
In a hut or
something.
I don't need
to write
in a powerful
nation.
I don't believe
in powerful
nations
anyway.
I could live in
Honduras, say,
on a beach—
live on
beans and
rice.
I could live in
a third-world
country with
a bicycle.
No doctor's
appointments.
(If you eat
beans and rice
and some fish
you probably
don't need
doctors
anyway.)
I could live in
a third world
country that
has no army
where I could
write nothing,
walk and bike
places to write
nothing and
send the things
I write
nowhere.

## A POEM

The time
we spend
in front of
screens
is time
away
from
love
and
nature
and
dreams.

# AUGUST 18, 2007

It was right for Max
to go to Argentina.
It just seemed right
to hug him at the
airport—for him to go
to see the world and to
live in Argentina and
see the country
for a year.

It was right for this
boy turning 17
to want to go away
to live in another
country and speak
another language.

It was right for us
to feel like we were
about to get on a
rollercoaster ride—
to be numb and sad
and happy at once.
We lived 16 years
of any advice
there was to give.

When he was 2,
before he could talk,
we climbed the
rocks and threw
handfuls of pebbles
one by one
into the Atlantic Ocean.

# POETRY CONTEST

If I was judge in a poetry contest
I would choose the most simple,
genuine poem which
sounds like a person talking or
dreaming.
Maybe it would have rain
in it and a red cat.
I would like to judge
the kind of contest where
a poem has a gypsy and a canoe
and an old hat and a cool August
day.
In this award-winning poem
a kid reads Lord of the Flies
and another kid asks
if jellyfish have brains and can you
ever stop thinking.

## MORE ON
## POETRY CONTESTS

Poetry contests have nothing
to do with poetry.
Poetry contests are about
money.
I wonder if Charles Bukowski
ever won any poetry contests.
Poetry contests are about
selling poetry magazines
to all of the losers
and the mothers
of the winners.
I would like to see a poetry
contest that does not want
you to send in poems but
instead some truthful writing
or just the money.

## TEACHING WRITING
## IS SIMPLY THIS:

First you get some paper
and a pen.
Then you get a book and
read it.
Then you talk about it
or anything.
Then you write about it
or something else.
This is all you need
to know.
It is a long path to get
to this simplicity.

# PLAY

My son slides down the hill
on the orange sled over patches
of ice and snow.
The neighbor's dog barks at him.
He pays no attention.
He stamps and walks through
the puddles that have formed
at the bottom of the hill.
He slides on the blue ice.
His boots soak through
to his socks.
He picks up a stick, marches
through the deep puddles,
splashes and digs trenches
and lines.
He wears red gloves.
A train goes past.
I watch from the
kitchen window
his vast imagination.
A stick and ice and puddles
and mud and he is good
for the afternoon.

# OCTOBER

October calls to my blood
to go with an acting troupe
in wagons and horses to villages
in New England valleys
that is the taste of apples
which touch the top of our caravan
and we pick as we pass
and bite into apples.
We set up stages in the wind.
Leaves fly around our horses.
We put on gypsy costumes
or rags or  become kings
and ladies with simple lines
and press our faces together
and breathe each other's breaths
and October air
and run into great embraces
and there are flashes of violence
with October afternoon sun across
trees and faces and swords and faces
of the people who are with
us in their imagination in our play—
our play.
O, it is good to long for a girl
I can never have,
to see her face looking up,
loving me.

# THE TRUTH ABOUT THE BEATS

Did you ever think that maybe the Beat poets were not so great
and that it was just a stream of consciousness trick that sounded
good because the lonely images strike us and the thoughts of one
human being jammed in words on pages I suppose is poetry
enough to readers and listeners half reading and half listening
because who listens to poetry wholly really come on let's face it
poetry is small potatoes, peanuts, it's the cheap side show
the menagerie they banned but anyone who saw one will not
forget the giant sitting up there looking slow and fleshy and sad
on his big chair as people streamed by staring streaming like
streams of images and thoughts and dreams and what the giant
was thinking in his giant brain with his big heavy lips as thick
as swollen giant lips.  But oh the stream of consciousness poets
love to suffer and light cigarettes in dark alleys and howl at
the moon and climb trees to stars and stand in doorways
of cheap Chinese restaurants like in good bad detective novels
on the trail of something like yourself and the girl like Veronica
Lake with Saxophone music--John Coltrane or maybe Miles
Davis or Dizzy Gillespie and never Louis Armstrong or Count
Basie.  And it is never middle-aged with kids for some odd
reason somehow the amazing thing about kids never got to
the Beats except for Gary Snyder but he doesn't count as a
Beat because, well, just because.  And the small compact
beautiful miracle missed them.  Oh, sure it is swell to be in a
smoky cafe reading and smoking and writing in a million
journal books and driving on America and all that but nothing
beats, I mean nothing beats it when your eight year old keeps
his own journal and you read it and it says, "I am happy."

# ENVIRONMENTALISTS ARE COMPLAINING

"The universe consists of nature and the soul."
--Ralph Waldo Emerson

Five-hundred thousand
acres of arctic wilderness
is now open
for oil exploration and drilling--
arctic marshlands.
The report was on the radio,
The oil companies
are heading north.
Do you realize
what that means?
The reporter ended
the story with these words:
"Environmentalists
are complaining."
Business tears
apart the earth
and the reporter says
environmentalists
are complaining.
Environmentalists
are complaining.
Yes, that's it,
we complain
and then we're going
to cry about it.
We complain and cry.
The arctic will become
a wasteland
and we will cry.
I guess it's okay
because the government
voted on it,
it must be all right.
They know what
they're doing.
Thoreau said:
"In wildness
is the preservation
of the world."
Emerson said:
"The world is so
beautiful that I

. . .

99

can hardly
believe it exits."
It doesn't
matter what they said.
Nice quotes, but
meanwhile....
Business is going
to build a Wal-Mart
on marshland
in Chesapeake Bay--
but environmentalists
are complaining.
I mean you can
build a Wal-mart
anywhere.
Can you ever
get back marshland?
"In wildness
is the preservation
of the world."
I wrote it on the
cinder block stage wall of
Winthrop Elementary School.
I wrote it with black
paint in two foot letters
while teachers lined up
children, waited for
quiet, kept them quiet
and orderly and in
lines--everything
in neat lines with
orderly lines, no woods
to play and get lost in
some made up game--
plenty of concrete
with lines and sports
and scores and teams

and lines and measuring
and keeping scores
and measuring.
The fact
that there are no
straight lines
in nature
doesn't matter.
No free-spirits running
no free-spirit wildness,
only order organized
statisticized numbered--
controlled.
The government
says it's okay.
They voted on it.
It must be all right.
They know what
they're doing.
The children have
to get in lines
and eat at this
time and be done
at that time and
get back in line.
No time for outdoor
free play--it
gets in the way
of academics.
Everything is for the future.
The future is what matters.
The principal didn't like,
"In wildness
is the preservation
of the world."
Shouldn't it be wilderness?
It was the wildness.

• • •

School knocks
the wildness
right out of you--
the free spirit
wildness to run
in fields and
woods and beaches
and turn around until
you are dizzy
with the joy
of being alive
is knocked out of you.
The government
said it's okay.
They voted on it.
They voted
to go to war.
It must be all right.
They know
what they're doing.
I think I'm going to go
out of my mind.
If you spend your days
riding your bicycle or
walking in the woods
they call you a loafer
like Thoreau. But if you
go to the arctic for oil
you are industrious,
ambitious, well employed,
downright American.
"The universe consists
of nature and the soul."
"In wildness
is the preservation
of the world."

We write about it
for each other.
We talk about it
for each other.
Meanwhile
Maybe the fact that
extinct means forever
doesn't matter?
Maybe arctic foxes
don't matter?

# DEER

Why do we
count
the deer
in a field?
We see deer
in a field
through
some trees
and we
count them—
eight.

# ZEN HERE

I do
not want
things
or money
or fame
because
I have
them.
I am
happy
with this
paper
and pen.

## SENRYU & HAIKU FROM SCRAP PAPER & FOUND POEMS

Clouds move across
a full moon. I let
   Mosquitoes bite me.

A butterfly
lands on a thing then
   something happens.

I ride home,
lean my bicycle on
   the white fence.

These poems
are two neat.
   Spit on them.

Painting goes nowhere.
It takes discipline to
   be irresponsible.

If there's one thing
I know about women
   it's nothing.

After you die a
butterfly lands on a thing
   then something happens

Cheap hotel,
high school reunion
   Why go back?

High school reunion
who are these people?
   Mars fades.

Crows are
happy-go-lucky. Ravens
   are devil-may-care.

Poetry is not important.
Write something
   truthful.

Life is not a syllabus.
A dragonfly lands on a thing
then something happens.

Max says he wants to
go fishing, catch fish,
eat them.

I need these things:
hat, bicycle, notebook
pen, time.

I hate to break it
to you dad but you don't
sing like Frank Sinatra.

The sun!
I will write
about it.

I go there
to leave and
come back.

This feeling
comes back and
goes away

Thoreau loved
cats for their
independence.

Seagull footprints
on the
football bench.

Sam explains
the universe
to the cat.

• • •

It is good to
go places
  by bicycle.

All thoughts of
the college student
  are beer.

Sometimes I
want to be employee
  of the month.

Sometimes I'm for
this. Sometimes I'm
  against it.

I growl and growl
you purr and purr
  which means yes.

I would like school
if we didn't have
  homework.

Walking home
daydreaming, looking
  around, talking.

When I read Frank
O'Hara the cat leaps
  into my lap.

Wars do nothing
for the people who
  die in them.

It is good when
authorities take little
  notice of you.

There was
something beautiful
    about today.

    I go to work because
it is an excuse to
    ride my bicycle.

There are old guys
who work outside
and fix things
their whole life

    If  I robbed a bank
would I
    lose my job?

    If  I  robbed a bank
I would get away
    on my bicycle.

    Denise changes the
the furniture. I like
    it no matter where.

    Three days of rain.
It's a good thing
    I'm not depressed.

    You dreamed I won
the Pushcart Prize.
    Better than winning.

    Max took a long walk
in the snow. Sam and I followed
    his footprints.

                                    • • •

How many fifty-five
year olds ride their
    bicycle to work?

My brother had a friend
named Warren whose father
    ate Spam--loved it.

Sometimes I am
supposed to be someplace else. It takes
    character to be irresponsible.

We used to live
a few houses behind underworld
    boss Frank Costello.

Snow on the
bottom of
    the canoe

We drift
in the canoe
    and yawn.

We sit by
the fire
    and yawn .

# ONE NIGHT

It is important to
listen
to a bad radio
and stay up too late
on a Saturday night
to be the last one
to bed.
The fire goes
out and the room
gets cold, the house
creaks this December
night.
I read
William Stafford and
write about now.
Sinatra until midnight.
I fall asleep on the
couch
feet way up.

# THE ZEN WOMAN

Like the beautiful Zen student
she came here and the boys fell
all over each other in serious love
with her because Eros was running
amuck--enamoring all of them.
"Her life was saturated with
the kind of beauty that
makes trouble."
In the story of the Zen woman,
she was kicked out of monasteries--
she drove the monks crazy and the priests
and their wives especially.
Later she burned down a 500 year
old temple with kerosene because
one wife's accusations ruined
an honest monk.
Men went mad as did the beautiful
Zen student.
Now, here, the boys want to know
everything about her.
It's like Aphrodite has come to this
third-rate college with her long thighs
and long eyes.
The boys fall over each other, drinking,
thinking about her--looking at their wives
and girlfriends and wondering.

# SAM'S QUESTIONS

Do I look Greek
or Roman
or Sumerian?
Do they ever
have their bows
slung around
them like this?

# PROSE AND POETRY

Some people say
that if you write
a paragraph
and break up
the lines like
a poem that it's
not a poem.
Funny, I say
it is a poem.
Take a paragraph
from any textbook
on any subject--
bust up the lines--
it's a poem.
It is words,
it has meaning,
it was written
by a person.
Frank O'Hara said
what he writes
is poetry because
he is a poet.
What's the difference
between prose
and poetry?
Beautiful writing
is beautiful writing.

# POEM

I like to say
I lived in
Port Washington
because I like
the sound
and image
of the words
Port Washington.
I like to say
I was born in
Manhasset
because I am
of the Manhasset
tribe of
Indians.

# RAINY RAIN DAY

This rainy rain

day when it
does not stop

is better than

anything
I can write--

anything
I can do.

# THE DAY AFTER
# THE FIRST DAY OF SUMMER

Watching it rain through the
open garage door
I think how everything in my life
has led up to this point.
I look through the deep trees across
the street.
There was a full red moon last night.
This morning I started to mow the lawn
and it began to rain. Now I sit in the
garage watching the rain and
thinking about my life. I sit here
with half of the front side mowed.
Rain forming puddles and the
railroad warning bell clanging,
then it stops. Cars drive past.
The rain is steady, pattering
on the driveway. It is the kind
of rain that makes you think
about your life. Yesterday was
the longest day of the year.
There was a full red moon last night.
Yesterday afternoon,
Max rode his bicycle to the library
by himself for the first time--alone
in the world. He took out books
on Portugal, Spain, Romania, Lithuania,
Greece, Argentina, and
The Reduced Shakespeare DVD.
When I came home last night,
Max was laughing and
Sam had just finished reading
Charlotte's Web
for the second time and he
went around the house quoting
Templeton the rat:
"What a night! What a night!"
What a last line in a book!
"It is not often that someone
comes along who is a true friend
and a good writer.  Charlotte was both."
There was a full red moon last night.

# DECEMBER 3, 2002

I am sleeping and sore
on the couch with my legs
way up on cushions and
I hear the telephone ring
and hear her footsteps
upstairs and hear her
talking.  My head is by
the window.  It is cold
and good and there
are tree limbs and
branches, gray and
yellow in the morning
sun.  I do not know
whether I am twelve or
forty-nine, home from
school, aching and
sleeping I think I see
me outside, the radio
wagon and pile of leaves
smelling like earth.
It is my mother's voice
upstairs or my wife's.
A record is over but the
needle is still on it
ticking and ticking.
The room is bright with
time, with now, and the
nowness is the same.
I am home from school
and home from school.
"Kindly excuse Danny
from school today…"
I am Sergeant Preston
of the Yukon in the
backyard standing on
my brother's Flexible Flyer.
Husky dogs through the
snow.  Bright dreams.
I hear dishes and pots
and things, a cheerful
voice on the radio.
Half sleep sweating.
Wood floors, smooth ceilings.
The telephone rings then stops.

# A BEAUTIFUL HOAX

November 1968. Southampton, New York. Friday night. Red moon over the ocean you could see from the potato fields. We were in the ballroom of the Merrill House (where James Merrill lived when he was a boy) at Nyack Prep School assembly concert to hear The Daphne Hellman Trio—harp, guitar and another guitar. There were150 boys from 13 to 18 years old, in striped school tie and school blue blazers and gray trousers, neat haircuts, sitting in folding chairs in rows. Great organ pipes on the back wall—organ on the other side. Stained glass windows from floor to ceiling like some middle ages place. A fireplace you can stand in. There was great oak paneling carved and rich. Everyone thought the music was hokey, like easy listening jazz and lugubrious arrangements. I happened to have liked it. Something happened. After each song the boys applauded louder and cheered and went wild. The goofy musicians in white tuxedos and Daphne in her evening gown, some sheer blue affair, blonde hair to her white shoulders and looking like some combination of an aging Grace Kelly, Veronica Lake, Katherine Hepburn, and Lauren Bacall, were glowing and beaming and grinning with big teeth and playing intensely. They probably never had a more enthusiastic audience. It was real for me. The rest were faking it. The musicians believed it. We made them happy. But it was all so beautifully false, 150 boys, all in on a wonderful spontaneous hoax.

# SUNDAY MORNING

Sometimes everything
is sad--
The sparkly little purple
dress in the
window of the storefront
dance school
The fancy bicycle
in the shop
The closed café
where they have
bad poetry readings
The comic book store
with the dusty
superman dolls
Everything is sad--
even jazz
Sometimes everything
is sad--
The cobbler shop
with the wooden
shoes--one says
Heineken's Beer
Cat's Paw sign
The smiling young
couples holding
babies, kids walking
behind them--
one girl has big feet
The frames you
buy with pictures
of happy people you
throw away
The China Buffet
Restaurant with the
mural of the Great Wall
The fresh smell of
oil paint of the white
front stoop and blue
door of the Mission
Church: "A Loving
Pentecostal Church
Flowing in the River
of the Holy Spirit "
You can hear the
spirit inside

The alley between
the Catholic Church
and the YMCA
The kids throwing
grapes up into
the sky as high as
they can and then
catching them in
their mouth.

## TUESDAY
## JANUARY 10, 2006

I took out a book on
Confucius and one
on Paul Klee
at the library and a
biography of Thoreau
and a book about
the reindeer people
of Siberia.
Max rode his bicycle
to the library
when I got home.
He said it was a good
day to study
languages.
Sam said it was a good
day to play and that
this is a good place
to see the sunset.

# SUICIDE

I figured
out today
that I
will
probably
never
kill
myself
because
there are
too many
interesting
hats
and bicycles
and drums
and canoes
in the
world
and I
no longer
have to
take
algebra.

# DRIFTING

When I am old
I will drift in
my canoe
and read
my old journals
about when
my sons
were children
running
barefoot--
and think
about life.

# WIDE IN PARIS
--Poem by Juan Gelman
translated by Maxfield Scott Sklar

What I miss is the old lion from the zoo,
we would always go for coffee in the Bois de Boulogne,
he would tell me of his adventures in Southern Rhodesia
but he was lying, it was clear he had never left the
Sahara.

In any case I loved his elegance.
his way of cringing his shoulders when faced with the little oddities
of life,
he  used to look at the French through the café window
and would say ´´the idiots have children´´.

The two or three English hunters he had eaten
stirred up bad memories and even melancholy in him,
´´the things one does to live´´ he would say
looking at his mane in the reflexion of the coffee.

Yes, I miss it very much,
he never paid for the drinks,
but he indicated the tip to be left
and the waiters greeted him with a special respect.

We said goodbye to each other at the bank of dusk,
He returned to son bureau, as he called it,
not without first warning me with a pat on the shoulder
´´be careful, my son, of Paris by night´´

I truly miss him deeply,
sometimes his eyes would fill with the desert
but he knew how to keep quiet like a brother
when, excited, excited,
I talked to him about Carlitos Gardel

# POETRY IS JUST NOT THAT IMPORTANT TO ME NOW

I just want to clear off my desk,
listen to jazz and write and write
and type and type about things
that are important to me at this
moment like the fact that my
son is 17 and in Catamarca,
Argentina for a year learning
tango and violin and my other
son is 11 and singing and playing
the flute and taking the bus to
school every day and the fact that
I ride my bicycle to work—even
in the rain, are the things on my
mind right now, and how Denise
is loving the movement work she
does and how I think about how it was
always great when Lionel Hampton
was on the Ed Sullivan show or
Johnny Carson whose three sons
I went to prep school with and can
picture them playing soccer in my
mind like every moment in my life
and every haircut like the one I got
in a hotel barbershop in New York
before my mother and I went to see
a play about Benjamin Franklin
with Robert Preston another time we
went to The Mikado and the Ice Capades

I was ten or eleven and at the Museum
of Natural History a new pair of trousers
was stolen from the trunk of our car.
We went to the top of the Empire State
Building. We ate at Longchamps
Restaurant. There were white table
clothes and my mother had a whiskey
sour. I was thinking of New York
when I was 11 and how I walked
and took the subway by myself all
over Manhattan and Brooklyn and
how now I feel compelled to write
about it. Before the bus came this
morning, Sam played flute and then
he sang "Amazing Grace" and
"Simple Gifts." He walked to the bus
stop with his backpack filled
with books and pencils.

. . .

# AS OF SEPTEMBER 19, 2007

I painted apartments in NYC
and went to acting school
then NYU for a master's degree
where my bicycle was stolen
at Washington Square Park.
Denise and I were married
in 1981. She is a dancer.
I drove a taxi and continued
to paint and did some writing.
In 1987, we moved
to Massachusetts
where I started another painting
business and got a teaching job
at this college. After a year they
offered me a full-time job
teaching creative writing
and some literature.
That was 20 years ago
and I still love teaching

and I'm a full professor.
We have two boys.
Max is 17 and speaks Spanish.
He spent time working
in an orphanage
in Honduras and is in
Argentina for a year on
an exchange program.
He plays saxophone, piano,
and accordion.
We play in a jazz band together.
He's also been in the
Rebel Shakespeare Co. since
he was ten!
He was King John in a school
play last year.
He also played Richard III.
Sam is 11 and plays flute
and also acts with the Rebel Co.
He was in The Tempest last year
and was Edward R. Murrow in
a school play this year.
He was in Macbeth this summer.
They're happy kids
and I manage to keep
them laughing.
I ride my bike to school
every day—seven
miles each way.

. . .

# A BRIGHT HOUSE FILLED WITH MUSIC

I am just a person
with a job to do
I am just a person
who needs to drift
in a canoe.
I am just a person
who needs to
mow the lawn.
I never get bored.
I am just a person
you see sitting
in a garage because
it's too complicated
in the house and
the bicycles and
tools and cars
are just that.
I am just a person
you see riding
a bicycle somewhere.
I am just a person
thinking things
through you will
never know
unless you read
what I write
about a woman
who loves
to be kissed
and wants to
be kissed
because romance
is important.
I am just a person
sad about
many things
so I listen
to sad music.

Children grow up
and go, but before
our house was
filled with them
and their friends
and light and
music and singing.
But I don't want
to end this with
singing. I want to
end where I am
just a person you
see sitting in a
garage as you go by.

# WHAT CRICKETS SAY

August crickets
August crickets
Cool August
August cricket
Cricket August
Nights and days
August crickets
telling each
other to love.

What do I want to write about today? I
need to mow the lawn at least one more
time before the leaves fall. Jack came
over last night, all excited about a poetry
reading he went to with some old famous
poet who rhymes like mad and who Max
and Sam and I make fun of, but I didn't
want to tell that to Jack, he was so glad
about the whole thing—how the old poet
signed his book for him and how he was
such a wonderful reader—clear and slow
for everyone to hear—probably because
of all of the old folks in the packed li-
brary audience. A young man gave up
his seat for Jack. It makes me sad that
so many people like that kind of crafted
poetry—there is nothing free about it and
I love freedom in life and in poetry. Oh
well. And besides, I don't like how this
old famous poet is a snob against free
verse and he said the free verse poets
were "stewing in their own juices." He is
stewing in the juice of a thousand dead
poets and dead poetry. Anyhow, Max and
Sam laugh about his clichés and contrived
phrases and that's what is important to
me—that my kids see how fake it is, how
artificial, how it is not natural and spon-
taneous and from some real deep place
instead of from some superficial technical
poetry trick place. I guess people have
different ideas of poetry—that's ok, those
are mine. The truth is I don't like po-
etry—I really don't—unless it is as natural
as the sun and moon and every tree on
the planet earth and everything in the At-
lantic Ocean, as free and chaotic as wild
places. It's wild places I am after—where
there is no human control. That's it—it's
all that control in those poems—I want
out of control—wild—untamed poetry.

• • •

There is too much authority in those poems. I want poems that are against authority. I do not want official poems—official sonnets—official villanelles—official couplets, which are almost impossible to write without hackneyed rhymes. I want unofficial poems with no authority. I don't want to be called a poet.

Some will say don't worry about it. Poet has such lousy connotations to me. Oh well. I would rather people say about me that he rides a bicycle to work and goes out on his canoe sometimes with his kids and plays drums in a jazz band when all the other drummers are busy. He's the last one they call. The fact of the matter is I'm just not that interested in poetry and writing except writing for myself. I mean it, writing isn't that important to me. So why write at all? Write to remember all of these bright days.

P.S. The poet was Richard Wilbur.

# UNTAMED LISA

Dear Lisa,
They write things and they say things about you, but they don't know
the truth. They don't know what love is. Talk about passion. Talk
about romance. Talk about love. Talk about sacrifice. You know
what a man wants. You know how to love a man. You did it for love.
No one understands that. Whenever I hear that song by Tom Jones I
think of you—you know the one—"She's a Lady." You are that lady.
I want to sing it to you. Love always, Roy

Dear Lisa,
I think of how you drove all that way for your man and I think that
that is love. You were probably listening to the radio. I wish I knew
what songs you were listening to and singing. I bet one of them
was that Helen Ready song "I Am Woman" because that is what you
are—pure woman. You know how to love a man. I hope they are
not sending you to therapy or something, because if they are they are
wrong. Is loving too much the act of a madwoman? And if it is, I say
more power to you.
Love again from, Roy


Dear Lisa,
The space program lost its greatest astronaut, you. I mean what
could be more important than love in space? I would like to go up
into space with you. I would like to kiss you in space. I would like
you to kiss me in space. We could kiss each other in space. Could
you imagine floating together in space and kissing—I mean, our lips
all swollen with blood and pressing against each others. Boy! That
would be something. With all my love, Roy


Dear Lisa,
Some of them say you have snapped. I don't believe this at all. They
say you have "unresolved issue" and have "lost perspective." I say
you see things exactly as they are. When a person loves someone,
nothing else matters. That's the power of love. I say, they have
"unresolved issues." They don't understand what it means to love
someone—I mean really love someone. They are all talk. There isn't
a pure and primitive and natural bone in their body. They have lost
touch with their pure and natural instincts. You should get a medal
for what for what you have done—shown the world the depth of
your love and passion. I for one am with you.
I'll love you always, Roy


Free Lisa!

• • •

Dear Lisa,
They say it was a love triangle, but I say they are wrong. She couldn't possibly have loved him the way you did. They call it attempted murder. I call it setting things right. You were right to do what you did. Oh, Lisa. Can't you see what I am trying to say. I would not betray you. I would never do the things he did. There was no triangle because that implies that two were in love with one. No. It was one in love with one and that is the way it would be with you and me. You have murdered me for love with you and I say that you have kidnapped my heart, Lisa, and I want to have the chance to prove it to you.
Deeply in love, Roy


Dear Lisa,
You look great in a trench coat—very sexy.
In true love, Roy

P.S. I love the way you look in the mug shot. I love the natural desperate woman look. The photos of you as an astronaut are fake. I see the smoldering passion behind those eyes. I love the earthy and wild untamed Lisa.

# WALKING

When I retire
I will give
away my
car
and walk.

# CREATIVE WRITING IS
# ECSTATIC SADNESS

"I'm heartbroken—doesn't anyone get
creative writing around here?"

Creative writing is what I don't know
about you
and what you don't know about me
and what I figure out about myself
and you and everything that is the
ecstatic sadness
which makes us the same.
Creative writing is scholarship of the soul.
(There's plenty of scholarship.)
It is research of the heart.
(There's plenty of research.)
Creative writing is the fact
that its outcome is wisdom.
(There are plenty of outcomes.)

Does The Diary of a Young Girl
need a bibliography?
(There are plenty of bibliographies.)
Do Mozart and Vivaldi and Leonardo
Da Vinci & Michelangelo need endnotes?
(There are plenty of endnotes.)
Does Bach need anything but his music?

Writers spill their guts and bleed inner life
on paper in public on the floor. It's a mess.
If you don't want to get dirty,
keep away.
Creative writing is how sometimes you
have to spit in the eye of the world.
Creative writing is you think you dreamed it.
Creative writing is the fact that we
cannot quantify love, even though we do

it all the time; and it is how things
you write will get you in trouble.
It is everything you do,
even the good things.

# CATS ARE LIKE THOREAU

They come and go
as they please.
Cats are like Thoreau.
You cannot explain them.
Cats are like Thoreau.
Everyone has their
own idea of them.
Cats are like Thoreau.
They mean something
different to anyone
who studies them.
Cats are like Thoreau
in the woods and
on the beaches.
They move like
themselves in the night
owning the world.
Cats are like Thoreau,
independent
like the practical
stars and moon.
Cats are like Thoreau
writing like a cat
and its tail.
Cats are alone
like wearing
a hat while drinking
orange juice.
Cats are like Thoreau
because people who
know them
like people
who know Thoreau
think of him
think of cats
think of Thoreau
and his flute
outdoors like a
cat in the mind
of the world.

# GRADES

CREATIVE
WRITING GRADING:
KURT
VONNEGUT
GETS
A+
DAN
SKLAR
GETS D-

# THANKSGIVING

"I cannot imagine  a God who rewards
and punishes the objects of his creation,
whose purposes are modeled after our own—
a God, in short, who is but a reflection of
human frailty." –Albert Einstein

Why do people want God to love them?
Why should God love people?
Why do people need to be loved by some
All-powerful being?
To say that God is about love
makes no sense to me because if
God was about love there would be
no suffering in the world.
Children would not suffer—
it's as simple as that.
What does it mean to love God so that
God will love you? What is that?
What kind of universe is that?
Sunday morning I stopped my bicycle
at the front door of a church in town
where I could hear the sermon from
outside. I sat on the bike, my foot
on the step and listened in the sunshine.
It was about God's "extravagant love."
The minister told a story about how
they gave pies to some orphans and
how he sensed from their expressions
that they knew they were loved, an
extravagant love, like God's love.
Then he told the congregation that
when you have pie at Thanksgiving,
think of God's extravagant love
for you.

. . .

I am listening in the open air
thinking those orphans were happy
to have pie, were glad someone cared
enough to give them pie. I don't believe
they were feeling anything to do
with God or God's love is like pie.
I think it's a lousy metaphor.
Why should God love us anyway
no matter what we do?
Because someone tells us?
Because we love God?
I realize how important it is that
people love one another, especially
enemies. But all that God's love idea
reminds me of the mess in the world—
war, famine, genocide, hate, despair....
These things are not about God's
extravagant love. Oh, sure, you could
say we are supposed to
use God's love on each other.
Face it—God is not about love.
God does not love us the way we
love pie on Thanksgiving.

# CHICAGO

I want to be asked to read poems in Chicago.
I want to take a train to Chicago and fall in
love on the way.
I want to spend time alone with you in a
hotel in Chicago.
I want to listen to you in Chicago.
I want to be heading to Chicago looking
for trouble.
I want my life to be a mess in Chicago
and read poems there with you waiting
for me in a hotel room and then to wait
for you in a little hotel bar.
I want to sit in a cool restaurant and look
into your eyes, with you wanting me to stare
into them.
I want to be like a guy in a play drinking
whiskey and it is good.
I want to sit around with you in Chicago
doing nothing.
I want to put my lips on your neck and
on your lips and you want me to put them
there.
I want to think about The Jungle and see
the rail yards and the Art Institute and think
about John Dewey and prohibition.
Chicago is where I want to read my poems.
Chicago is where I want to look for trouble,
find it, and  have a love affair with you.

# NO POEM HERE

This poem is not going to give advice
or be wise or tell you how to run your life
or give you tips on how to write a poem
or make love or how to get a job or date
and what to say and do on it or how to
take care of your lawn. This poem will
not give you anything useful—nothing to
remember—nothing you can be tested
on—no great insights into anything.
This poem will do nothing for your career
advancement. You can't put the fact of
it on your resume. You probably already
feel cheated by it. Stop reading it now.
I fell down the stairs writing it so I got
a twisted ankle out of it. This poem will
not give you any important information.
There is no information in this poem—
no deep philosophy, no shallow
philosophy—no philosophy at all.
You cannot sell this poem or use it in
businesses let alone frame it and put
it on a wall in your office or give it
to your mother. No one will quote
this poem in a speech—no old poet
will quote it to say something
about poetry. This poem won't get you
on TV or in the movies or make you
famous or better looking than you are
or smarter or more attractive to the
opposite sex or the same sex, I guess.
This poem will not contribute to your
retirement, neither will it give you
discounts on a hotel room nor will it
give me literary merit (whatever that is).
Whatever you are after this poem
will not help. You won't feel anything
or even get a sense of anything
or learn anything from it.
There are no allusions to Greek myths—
no Artemis or Persephone or Penelope
or Prometheus or Aphrodite. Not one
muse in this poem, not even Thalia.
No catchy phrases or anything clever.
This is not a clever poem.

There are no metaphors here—
no Venetian blind shadows across
the floor and this paper. There is no
"coming of age" "state-of-the-art"
"cutting edge" anything in this poem.
This poem has no concerns or issues.
Brooklyn is not in this poem.
There is no history in this poem.
There is no course of action in it.
This poem doesn't want to control
anyone. This poem will not win
an award unless there is an award
for lying in a hammock with a hat on.
There is no craft in this poem.
The moon is not in this poem.
Mars is not in this poem.
No one has elegant eyes in it.
No one is run through with a sword
in this poem. No raccoons or bicycles
or chairs or tables thrown aside
from knocking someone's block off.
This poem will not make you happy
or sad or enlighten you, and even
if somehow it did enlighten you,
you would still be miserable.
God is not in this poem because
I like to keep God out of these things.
There are no rivers or canoes or maps
or windy winds or clouds or stars or
earth things. No ripples in a pond
signifying anything. There is no jazz
or social justice in this poem. No
children running and banging into
each other. No dogs, lists, panthers,
or actors here. Shakespeare is not
in this poem or quotes like
"All things are ready if the mind be so."
This is not a poem for broads

• • •

or  women or chicks or girls or cats or men
or boys or any particular season or time.
This poem wants nothing from you
and it gives you nothing.
You can take this poem into the
sauna with you, but why?  Why read
this poem again or even once
for that matter as a matter of fact
in my humble opinion.
There is nothing Zen about this poem.
It will not help you get published
and it will not knock your socks off.
There is no nature in this poem
unless it is a cigar.  There are
no childhood memories in this poem
like the first time you were left
alone and you waited the whole time
in the vestibule.  This poem is not
about freedom or liberty or independence
or responsibility or scotch whiskey
in fact this poem is irresponsible.
This is an irresponsible poem.
It's a cancelled policy due to
a late payment.  This poem is not
going to send you a letter on pink paper
telling you where you stand or how
you can do better but are falling
behind on the quizzes which
prove you have not done the reading
even though you may have.
To this poem, It doesn't matter
what you have or have not done.
Life doesn't have a syllabus.
This poem doesn't give a rats
behind what you do, I reckon.
This poem is here to fill pages
in my journal to finish it with words
like itinerary and beauty and potential
and bones.  This poem is not

about bones though it should be.
There are no feasts or music
or jumping in this poem.  There are
no Friday nights longing for you
in this poem.  Nothing is going
to happen in this poem. It will end—
no turn of thought—it will just be over.
It will not stop in an interesting
place and there will be no funny
that is that ending.  No image will
sum it up.  It will not end with trees
somehow. Neither Frank Sinatra nor Ella
Fitzgerald will sing in it.  Miles Davis
is not in it.  He wouldn't want to be.
This poem will not be submitted for
publication even though it will.
This poem will not be in a contest.
It will not sit in a café in Aztec,
New Mexico (1963 All-American City)
desert sun shining in. It is not a poem
about the desert.  There are no rattle
snakes
in this poem or WWI telegraphs.  No
horses or uniforms or signs in this poem.
This poem is the only thing
on a road in autumn.
This poem is on a train.
This poem is alone on a train.

## FOUND POEM FROM SEVENTEEN RULES OF POETICAL PILGRIMAGE #12

Do not become
intimate
with women
haiku poets;
this is good for
neither teacher
nor pupil.
If she is in earnest
about haiku,
teach her
through another.
The Way of Haiku
arises from
concentration.
Look well
within yourself.

# PAPER

When I see
blank paper
I want to cover
it with words
I don't know why
something in me says
life is big
write big.

# GRADING

Just because
you have a
formal
grading
management
system
doesn't mean
students learn
more or less or
that your
system
works.

# TEACHING

They turn you into
a  file clerk Nazi
record  keeper
pencil pushing
bureaucrat grader
judge of baloney
 & call it
"advising" and
"mentoring" and
"teaching."
(Some mentoring.)
I forgot to say fascist.
Did I mention Nazi?

# 1953

I read this article in
The Boston Globe
about this poet who
was born in 1953
the same year as me
and it said how he
won a Pulitzer Prize
and has very bad
depression and was
an alcoholic before
and took drugs too
and taught college
and got fired and how
his parents were divorced
and his father was a
famous poet too who
also won the Pulitzer Prize
and had bad depression
and hit his son, the poet
my age, and then the
mother remarried and
the stepfather hit the boy
too though he denies
he did it and now the
poet gets awards and
grants and fellowships
and poems in
The New Yorker Magazine
and poetry books published
left and right and there
were two years where
he couldn't leave his
apartment he was so
down but now his wife,
a poetry translator,
understands him and he
became Catholic and
works in a place where
he helps people and
kids too in trouble a lot
like the way he was.

# WHEN I WAS TWENTY-ONE

Once I met a girl on a train who wanted to have sex all the time. It was the thing she was most interested in doing. She was the caretaker of the 1770 House Inn which was closing for the fall, and since the owners were upstate, she had the place pretty much to herself that September; and the town basically closed up too. I could do it whenever she wanted for as long as she wanted. We stayed drunk most of the time. I had graduated from college and did not know what to do and since the pub in the basement was ours getting drunk and chain smoking Old Golds and having sex with this thirty- year-old woman seemed to make perfect sense. I got a job painting mansions on the ocean. It was a good job because you could be drunk and smoke and not worry about anything. The boys and me played a lot of ping pong in one summer mansion in Amagansett. It was good to work and screw and smoke and not give a damn about anything. The radio only picked up an easy listening station which was okay with me, especially when they played Jackie Gleason. There was no T.V. We were nobodies in the town. I had an old Peugeot bicycle. She had a 1963 Saab station wagon from her ex-boyfriend who was 42 and some sort of music business executive that did a record with Stevie Wonder and she had her name in the album. I guess we lived like that until some time after Thanksgiving; and the minute I started to get attached to her (which was really dumb and she was smart enough to know this) we were through. Besides, she was not interested in college boys. And to tell you the truth, after a while she stayed in her ratty white bathrobe, strummed her guitar all day, smoked cigarettes, ate nothing but A & P apple pies from the box, and quit taking showers. (We saved the Old Gold coupons and had a pretty good pile of them by the time we split up.) The Inn had no central heating. She went to New Jersey to see her mother. She said she'd be back but we both knew she wouldn't. I kept fires going in the fireplace, slept on top of the blankets so I never had to make the bed. I slept in my clothes. Electricity and water were shut. No one knew I was there. I went to the frozen beach and drank at night and stared at the stars and waited.

# OPPOSITE SKY

I like how that girl is always
eating.
She has a big glowy face.
We can write together.
We can write these things
are too beautiful. I am
after what is innocent
luminous and true.
The Indian Ocean and
everything in it.
Your purpose on earth
is to wander.
Your purpose on earth
is to get lost.
She is a splendid gypsy.
Gypsy first-class.
I'll write an important letter.
That's what I'll do!
Today I am a hungry bird.
Suddenly I am a canoe drifting.
This is an elegant grief.
If I told you once,
I told you a thousand times!
I'm efficient & organized &
a better poet than Robert
Frost but not better than
Walt Whitman.
How can you measure
luminosity?

# AN OFFICE

Sometimes I want to
have an office in a
professional building
downtown with
psychologists and
lawyers and dentists
and accountants with
their names on the
directory in front and
on their doors and
my name on
my door too, nothing
else, just my name.
And I can go to this
office and look out
the window at the
tree and write with
a typewriter and
there will be a black
rotary dial telephone
and a radio
with a red light.
I want to go to this
office to think
about you and write
about you and
dream about your
elegant wisdom.
If the telephone
rings it will be
a wrong number.
I will drive
by this office and
see my name on
the directory outside.
It will be a lonely
office and I will go
there Sunday nights
to listen to the radio.

# A DREAM

He had a dream
that he was having
a meeting with
her and it turned
out to be in her
bedroom.  She was
in the bed.
"I can come back,"
he said.
"No, come in.
This is where I'm
having meetings."
It was dark.
He couldn't see
her face, but her
voice was smiling.
The bed took up
practically the
whole room.

# HOW TO WRITE A COLLEGE PAPER

Use plenty
of therefores
and furthermores
and on the other hands
and moreovers
and hences
and thus
and considerings
and similarlys
and contrastings
and dreams.
Did I mention
myriad
and plethora
and dearth?

# JACK KEROUAC WANDERING

I wandered that morning after taking my son, Max, to Rebel Shake-speare rehearsal where he was playing Marcellus in Hamlet  I sat looking out at Marblehead Harbor.  A woman and her son went by in kayaks.  I thought how I could spend my days wandering and writing and listening to people.  I heard a woman at the next table in a café; she seemed to be in her early sixties.  She was talking about her daughter.

"There isn't a thing in the world I can do about it.  She's giving up her apartment in Miami—going to
New York—take voice lessons—get a place, an office job.  I thought she'd meet someone...." she said.

Max says I should write a poetry writing kit.  I like the idea of a kit—a How to Write Poetry Kit.

This is the town where I was wandering fourteen years ago waiting for Denise who was dancing, when a pick-up truck pulled over with two working guys and they were smiling and looking at me.

"Are you Jack Kerouac?" asked the driver and the passenger nodded.

Maybe it was my hat, the rucksack, the fact that I needed a shave?

"No," I said, "Jack Kerouac is dead—died in 1969." This was 1987.

At first I thought they were putting me on—but they didn't make a joke about it.

"He's dead?" the passenger said.

"We thought you were Jack Kerouac."You look like Jack Kerouac.  Sorry.  Bye." And they drove off.

It almost looked like they did this all the time—drive around telling guys they look like Jack Kerouac.  It sure made me feel good, though—especially since in college I read plenty of Jack Kerouac books.  I used to wander through the book stacks in the college library, read old issues of Time, The New Yorker, and
National Geographic.  Once I found this black book with this great title I'd never heard of before—On The Road.  I read it that day.  I got some of his other books and couldn't stop reading them—The Town and The City, Dharma Bums, The Subterraneans, Lonesome Traveler, Maggie Cassidy.  I tried writing like him—that beat spontaneous jazz prose stream of consciousness. It was great. It set me free.

I was steamed because everything becomes a dream, a memory—and it's time that does it.  I stopped reading Kerouac because I figured once you've read him, you've read him.  But I still dig him.  He was a wonderful wandering genius.

Kerouac used to say when he thought of New England, he thought of two fellas in wool shirts heading to work in a pick-up truck.

# JUST FOR THE RECORD

I am writing
this poem to
tell you that
I am a great
poet because
otherwise
you might
not have
figured it out.

# THE SIGNS (JAZZ SONG 4)

I miss the signs every time
The signs in your eyes
I miss the signs every time
we're together
The signs in the way you
look at me, the curl of your
lips, the way you sit long
and folded like a red cat.
I miss the signs because
I'm so busy wondering how
you could love me though
you give me the signs and
I miss the signs every time,
every time I am with you.

# METAPHORS

Your eyes are like your eyes
Your skin is like your skin
Your lips are like your lips
Your hair is like your hair
Nothing to compare your
beauty is your beauty.
Your legs are like your legs.
Your  arms and hands
and fingers and neck
and neck and neck...

# TALL BLONDE

I am suddenly
interested in
Hillary Brooke
because she
reminds me
of you &
when I am
with you I
feel like
Lou
Costello.

# THIS KID

Michael Quinn died of a heroin
overdose in 1970. They buried
him with his boots on and his
Grateful Dead tee-shirt, the one
with the skeleton and roses.
He was a klutzy kid with greasy
blonde hair and foamy saliva in
the corner of his lips
and he talked like he had
marbles in his mouth. For
Michael it was either college or
Vietnam--same for me. He was
a whiz at math, I mean, gifted
in it and got a math scholarship.
He lived  on East  7th Street with
his mother. Our friend Teddy
Kovak lived in the same tenement.
Kovak was a natural athlete.
They took heroin together some
times. I'd see them on the stoop,
Kovak's girlfriend too, at night
smoking Kool Cigarettes,
drinking 7UP.

# THIS IS THE LIFE

This is the life
Sammy says. We're
in the hammock

nothing like it
this spring
Saturday the

trees are treeing
kids are kidding
leaves are leafing

breeze, breezing
fence, fencing
sky, skying

the cool, cooling
the blue, bluing
flowers are flowery.

An aroma in the air
reminds me of spring
when I was a kid and

will remind Sam of
when he was a kid
when he grows up.

I close my eyes
on this hammock
on this happiness

open them, see Sam
and leaves and sky
dream of words
and jazz, someone

speaking Spanish
in the distance.

We float and drift
and dream in this
hammock, this
happiness.  I love
how Sammy says Dad.

He will have his
dad on this spring
hammock, this
spring happiness.

# MAXFIELD SCOTT SKLAR'S REVIEW OF DAN SKLAR'S HACK WRITER: STORIES, PLAYS, POEMS

"I've read worse.
Don't make me laugh.
Some poetry…
It ought to go in
the horror section
of the library."

# WILD LOVE SONG

Sometimes I am sad
sitting on the kitchen
floor, violin music
on the radio playing
old sad Bach, then
it gets happy.
Orange whistle on
the floor, refrigerator
hum, the ache of love
for you sleeping long
somewhere.
What do
you do with those
long legs at night?

# I PICTURE HER

I picture her
laughing now
with someone.
I picture her
writing now
about the
old west
like a white
cat
on
a typewriter.

# THE DESERT

It was actually now because back when
I was in college Al and Russ and I drove
to the Mustang Ranch whore house out-
side Las Vegas, Nevada—1971 I think
it was and we were 18 and happy as hell
about it—the desert was red about
it—hot and beautiful about it. I mean we
were getting a hard-on all over the place
about it just thinking about it, talking
about it speeding down long straight roads,
desert sun across our laps and faces,
drinking Coors Beer making sandwiches
from loaves of bread and cheese and biting
into apples singing "Mustang Sally" and me
thinking maybe I'll meet someone like
love at first sight for both of us and we
will live together in the desert with horses.
I was an idiot romantic even then.
It was out near small mountains of rocks
and looked like a big crazy ranch house,
like some bad dream neon lights motel.
I got this feeling in my stomach like nerves
like opening a Playboy Magazine only this
was real and you'd rather not, you don't
want to but you do because you have to—
The details don't matter. Russ and Al
were gone after two drinks at the bar
where I stayed thinking always thinking
with this dopey smile and incredible
desire. The perfumes, glimpses of panties,
thighs showing, wet lips, bare
shoulders, hands on me but eyes with
something off something not right
they looked at me and didn't, looked
inside themselves and at something
distant at once and each way was fuzzy.
"How about a date?" "Like a date?"
"Ask me on a date, would you?"
They called it a date and I was feeling
and thinking and thought about that later
on, a month, a year, five years—actually
now and I knew I had to say I didn't go
through with it and it had to be true
and I never  told anyone until now, at 47,
to this college creative writing class

• • •

when the topic of a whore house came up.
The boys in the class were whooping it up
as I told the story about how Al and Russ
came back to the bar kind of dreamy like
and very happy and the boys sighed when I
told them about me and the women
in the class were quiet—thinking.
I knew I would get married someday—
have kids, I mean I don't want to sound
so moral and all because I'm not,
in my mind sometimes like Jimmy Carter
and any man for that matter,
(I don't know about women).
I do know it was their eyes and the fact
that there was no one there for me
to love in the desert.

# JUNE 26, 1999, SAM SAYS

What do the rocks say?
What does the grass say?
What does the cement mixer say?
What does the pool say?
What does the day say?
The wind feels like cotton.
We like the wind.
What do the crickets say?

# SOME ANSWERS

The rocks say we hold the railroad ties.
The grass says we grow and like it.
The cement mixer says I mix cement.
The pool says I will cool you.
The day says I am hot and blue.
We like the wind on our face.
The crickets say we like this meadow.

# CANADA

I want to be
in Canada
wearing snowshoes
heading to some
lodge
and a fire,
to your lips,
to your long arms,
to the night.

## HAT

Thoreau's hat
was old
and weather-beaten
with plenty
of holes around
the brim.

# WRITING

I write unsolicited
manuscripts &
  put them in
    a pile of other
unsolicited
  manuscripts.
I wouldn't know
  how to write
   solicited things
unless it is about
  looking at the moon.

# LETTER EXPLAINING WHY I WANT TO SPEND SOME TIME AT AN ARTIST'S RETREAT ON AN ISLAND IN MAINE.

I want to be away from everyone I know and everything that is familiar to me. I want to wander and get lost in a place where nature, rather than human things, dominates the landscape. My writing and painting has been grounded in themes of society, civilization, personal, and professional. I want to see where the art goes when I have a distance from teaching and meetings and even loving my family. I want to spend time writing and painting and see how it works without thinking about things I have to do. Don't get me wrong, I love the commonplace errands of life. It is actually a joy for me to go to the post office, take my kids to music lessons, pick up milk, make breakfast, plan classes, read student papers, and go to work. I have been working on a book of poems and will continue to do so. I am also working on a series of portraits of poets and writers but am not tied to anything, I'll write or paint anything that comes up.

# FOR A TIME

Sometimes I feel compelled to write but I do not know what to write so I begin like this figuring that something will come to me and it does this sudden interest well not so sudden interest in union ideas and doing something for people rather than all this writing and painting and this sense of being anti-technology even though I am writing this on a computer looking at my old Royal typewriter I pull out now and then to hear it and smell it and write with it what would Thoreau think about a computer what I am thinking is if I could find Whitey Bulger there's a million dollar reward I quit the band today there are plenty of drummers around and I'm the only father to my boys I mean there's enough music in my life enough loneliness enough togetherness Thoreau said "It's wrong to systematize our thought and experience Let it be as it is contradictions and all" and it is liberty I am after even though I already have it I'm not out to lead anybody leadership implies control I don't want to control anybody tell them my way of doing things is anything but another way to do things electric screens imply control What would Walt Whitman do with a computer you think he'd sit there and say anything different you think he'd put his students in front of computers I tell you it's big brother it's Orwellian it's Kafkaesque metaphorical how schools are proud of their computer labs and make signs to tell you where they are I mean after all they're machines Shall we meet in room 125 I mean people are impressed with machines in educational settings how about a cotton gin room I like machines as sculptures I like old computers in the snow dirty old snow from December and it's February now and raining and perfect February time I think this summer I will pack the kids in the car and head north to some mountain and climb it look at the streams and rocks and sky and stay there for a time.

# SUMMER

When I tell people Max
was Duke Theseus in
A Midsummer Night's Dream
last summer and had great
lines like, "Never can anything
be amiss when simpleness
and duty tender it" and
"The lunatic, Lover, and poet
are of imagination all compact"
and that he learned his lines
in two nights up in his room.
"Oh, your son is a budding
thespian," they say. And I'm
thinking, no, he's just a kid
who was in a  Shakespeare play
last summer.  Besides, I hate that
budding young thespian crap.

# RUGGED

The poems in Poetry Magazine
are dainty, that's the word—dainty.
Even the poem with a man
looking at a woman's legs.
Too many flowers and regrets
and gardens and little churches
and music lessons and not
enough Malcolm X.
There aren't enough poems
that clobber you.
I been trying to tell you
If I told you once, I told
you a thousand times,
my poetry is rugged.
I tell you it's rugged.
I walk around my house
declaring it is rugged.
I reckon my poetry
is rugged.  It ain't dainty.
It's tough and rugged.
My wife says it's not
rugged.  I say it is dog-eared,
worn-out, beat-up, dog-legged,
left in the rain, and rusting
in the backyard all winter.
It's a busted stone wall,
a falling down fence.
There is nothing academic
about it I hope.
I say my poetry is rugged.
My kids say it's rugged too
because I tell them it is and
we all march through our house
saying it's rugged I tell you!
My wife says it's not.
I say it's a radio playing
in another room.

• • •

A car engine running.
A cold February night
with Jupiter and Venus
and Mercury visible
from home.
It's me thinking about
the FBI file on Malcolm X
and eating Shabazz Bean Pie
in Harlem on the street
with a Kool Cigarette
in the cold city air
thinking about Thelonious Monk.
It is Malcolm X wounded
then dead.
The only way to be yourself
is to be yourself.
I lose and it is good.

# MARCH WINDS

I fought the wind as a boy
delivering the Long Island Press
to development houses.
Solid Robin Hood three-speed
and me with crew cut pushing
through March winds, folding
papers and placing them in
mailboxes or screen doors of
little houses with patchy lawns,
each had its warm sour smell.
Wind pulled veins across the bay
where I stopped to have a Milky Way—
Fingers red and cold, wind
whizzing over my ears.
I waved to kids I recognized from
school but didn't know.
Delivered to the Republican Club,
puffy men in tight suits sat at
the bar.  I'd grab a handful of
peanuts, hop on my bike and race
up the pebbly driveway and
line of tall pine trees to tiny
houses where old men cooked suppers
at four in the afternoon.
O, the March wind stung my face.
The sun went down around six-thirty
when I put my bike in the garage.
Dinner smelled great and my dog,
Happy, jumped all over me.
I put hot water on my fingers
and face.
The lights sparkled like candles
and dinner was beef stew
and apple pie and cream.

# RAIN

Sometimes it is good
to stay in a motel
March in the rain
by the ocean
raining
in a town where
most everything is shut
down and it is good
to be in this motel
you stayed in before
when you were
not alone
and could not
watch rain.

# HE DREAMS OF SPAIN

He dreams in Spain
His dreams are in Spain
He dreams about Spain
He walks in Spain
in his dreams
He sleeps in Spain
in his dreams
He dreams in Spanish
in his dreams
He dreams he fought
from the mountains
in the Spanish Civil War
He dreams of the olive
fields and cork trees
He dreams of swimming
in the Mediterranean
the water blue and cool
He dreams of fishing on
Spanish beaches
He dreams of Cervantes
writing—Spanish sun
across the paper
He dreams of gypsies
barefoot with naked
babies on the grass
He dreams of empty
bull fighting rings
The memory of fights
He dreams of Catalan
nights with stars
He dreams of dreams
of Spain
He dreams of tapas
and windmills
and horses
and siestas and Flamenco
and Lorca and workers
and their caps
He dreams of tortilla
española and the Basque
country and Spanish
hills in the distance

# BIRD SANCTUARY
-Poem by Samuel Sklar

A certain spot in the woods
with a bridge on an algae
covered pond near a bush.
I stood, seeds in my hand
held up high above my head.
Still and silent I stood as
birds fluttered toward me.
One came at me, talons like
gentle clips on my hand,
and took a few seeds and
flew back to the bushes.
Around me I heard the
chirping and fluttering
of the birds and the
lapping of the pond.

# UNCLE JOE

Uncle Joe was crushed
by a truck. It was ironic
considering he had just
married at fifty-six because
he was finally in love with
someone (a blonde forty-
eight year old cashier at
Snow White Coffee Shop
on Kings Highway).
She wept and none of his
relatives believed her.
They could not see how
anyone could love Joe.
After all, he was a
bachelor and possibly
probably tough to live
with, with the portrait
of his mother straight
over the couch, and the
neat way he tucked
things in places, and how
he cooked his little suppers
of beans and bread,
and listened to Count Basie
too loud every night.
He mowed the small yard
with a manual lawn mower
and wore a brown fedora
and gray trousers.
But she made him happy
for fourteen months.
They were happy
and made each other
happy, even though
she chewed gum and
laughed too loud.
Joe's brothers and their
wives did not like her.
She did not go to college.
The fact that Joe never
went to college did not
matter. He was self-made.
With a Brooklyn trucking
business.

• • •

He paid off union officials.
He hollered at his men.
His face was a big piece
of concrete.
He was happy with Shirley
for fourteen months
and no one knew it
but Shirley.

## BRING STRANGE GIFTS TO AUTHORITY

Face it
no one
really
questions
authority
except
G. Tod Slone
and the
people
who send
him
poems.

# WRITER'S BLOCK

Either I have writer's
block or no time to write?
I'm not sure which.
And I cannot figure
out if I have any ideas
or not, but I think I do.
It occurs to me that
I want to be walking
alone in a blizzard, thinking
about being in a tea room
alone with you.  I don't mean
I want to do this, but I want
to want to do this while
walking in a snowstorm.

# THE FACT OF BICYCLES

The fact of canoes
the fact of bicycles
the fact of drums
the fact of rain
and farms and
Chinese Restaurants
rainy Sunday nights
across the street
from old train stations.
The fact of violins,
saxophones, and harps.
The fact of flutes
and the earth and
dreams and cold
and warm and
the fact of you
reading this fact of
poem—the fact
of your face—
the lines.
The fact of sky.
The fact of stars
the fact of nothing
the fact of bicycles
the fact of drums
the fact of canoes
the fact of farms
the fact of loneliness
that is good and
wants not
to be lonely.
The fact of wind.
The fact that "cameras
are present for your
protection."

• • •

The fact of freedom
the fact of endings
the fact of jazz
the fact of the sun
the fact of your lips
the fact of love
the fact of slow down
and love.
The fact of go.
The fact of how
we dream
about each other.